From Heart to Heaven

Esteban Antonio

PALM TREE
PUBLICATIONS
A Division Of
PALM TREE PRODUCTIONS

CW01521902

PUBLISHED BY PALM TREE PUBLICATIONS

A DIVISION OF PALM TREE PRODUCTIONS

KELLER, TEXAS, U.S.A.

PRINTED IN THE U.S.A.

Palm Tree Productions is a Media Services Company dedicated to seeing the Kingdom of God advanced by ministries and businesses with excellence, integrity and professionalism through the use of high quality media resources. Whether the publication is print, audio or visual, we are dedicated to excellence in every aspect from concept to final production.

It is our desire that this publication will enrich your life and cause you to increase in wisdom and understanding.

For more information about products and services available through Palm Tree Productions, visit our website at www.palmtreeproductions.net.

Manuscript Services, Cover Design & Layout by Wendy K. Walters, Palm Tree Productions

ISBN 13: 978-0-979580-1-7

ISBN 10: 0-9795480-1-2

To contact the author visit:

www.savespain.org

www.whitehorseministry,org

Table of Contents

Introduction

This book is intended to reveal who we are meant to be in the fullness of Jesus Christ. He is the true one and only Son of God — the Father of all creation. It celebrates the gifts He gave all of us in His death, resurrection and ascension to heaven when He sent the Holy Spirit — the Spirit of Truth and the Comforter. He brings ALL things to our remembrance.

In Paul's letter (Romans 8:15), the Holy Spirit is described along with many other gifts from God, the father of Jesus Christ. Paul speaks about the Spirit of Adoption (from which we call Abba, Father) and our spirit as we need to receive it — as part of the new birth in being born again. We must be saved in the salvation that Jesus won for us on the cross. We need a new heart to understand and to obey just as Jesus obeyed. We are meant to be just like Jesus, a Son of God and not just a creation of God. To do this we need to have both His Spirit and His heart. We must not operate from our own spirit and our own heart. Many books have been written on the Holy Spirit, but none I know cover this area. This book is written on the heart.

It is about the heart we were supposed to have from the very beginning. What is that heart? What is involved for us to have God's Spirit and God's heart in us? What does it mean to know the love of Christ (the love He had for us and the Father) that passes ALL knowledge?

The teaching which follows is a prophetic mandate. It was received in the form of a powerful ministry tool. The revelation can be applied to any ministry — whether it is music, art, pastoring, operating in the prophetic or the apostolic. It provides the key to more wisdom and understanding. In fact, it is relevant to anything revolving around the promises of God in the Bible for your life — especially Salvation. **From Heart to Heaven** is the first of two books. This one focuses on the Spirit and heart of God. My second book is focused on the area of music; its purpose and the power of the prophetic. It will reveal what music is and what happens when we play down the music from heaven. It will disclose where and when and who we are supposed to be when we create or make music. But before we can do these things, we must first see the Kingdom of Heaven, not just as Jesus spoke to Nicodemus in the Gospel of John (John 3:3), but to enter the Kingdom of Heaven deeply to bring its purposes down to earth. Jesus said when He taught us how we are to pray, "Thy Kingdom come, Thy will be done on earth as it is in heaven."

For this book, **From Heart to Heaven**, the Lord showed me that it was not just about doing His will in all that we do, it is also about who you are when you do His will and who you know yourself to be. In the area of knowing — in the place of receiving from God, the Lord Jesus and the Holy Spirit revolve totally around the **HEART**. For only when the heart of the Lord Jesus is fully formed in us will we be in the same area of relationship with the Holy Spirit. This will be the beginning, where we begin to walk as Jesus did, as He was when the Word was made flesh. For me, this is true praise and worship itself!

Just as God anoints understanding — that area of knowing in the heart, what this book teaches can be applied to any work of ministry for the believer. It even applies to the unbeliever in order that he may come to know the Lord Jesus. Once digested, the material in this book is itself a ministry to receive the total Presence of the Word in the heart.

As this teaching was freely given to me to bring a deeper awareness of the heart, this book on the heart is freely given. I want to make this tool available to everyone. I want the fullness of Christ in the Lord Jesus to be a blessing to many who want more. This book is a way to bless all those who do not know the Lord by first teaching how to localize the heart and then to show the importance of the church to the unbeliever as well as to the world. It is my desire to change their hearts, that they would trade in their hearts of stone for the heart of the Lord Jesus. Either we are in Him or we are not. For only when we are with Him can we be of one heart, one mind and one flesh "In Him."

THE VISION

At 12:00 midnight on the 14th of May, 2005, in Almunecar, Spain, I was in our house on the top of a mountain side when the Lord Jesus spoke to

The Lord spoke to me in a series of visions

me in a series of visions. These began back in Kensington, England in the last week of February in 1998. It was then that I was healed of an irreparably damaged spine and received the Holy Spirit.

Some of these visitations were open visions in which, at times, I was taken up to Heaven. Over a period of the next eight years, the Lord spoke to me and finally released me to write this book.

After I was miraculously healed, (and this miracle was observed by many people in the church of Kensington Temple, London) a prophecy was given to me by Debbie Holmes, the minister who prayed for me. She prophesied that the Lord wanted my music and would release me to go out and reach the lost. Shortly after this event, the Lord Jesus Christ appeared to me in a vision and told me that I must go to the Nation of Spain!

MY TESTIMONY

I was 3 years old in the year 1965 when I began to study the guitar. In 1971, at the age of nine years, I entered the Royal College of Music as one of the youngest students to be accepted. By the age of 11, I was the youngest person ever to perform the Aranjuez Guitar Concierto. Since then, I have toured from Japan, around the world to Canada and throughout Europe. I have been involved in the production of music and composition for television and film as well as for live performances with various orchestras and dance companies as well as for solo events.

The guitar became my world and my god – that is until I realized there was more to life than this.

~~~~~~~~~~~~~~~~

It wasn't until I suffered a terrible accident that left my spine with irreparable damage that I began to ask the question, "Who was this man Jesus Christ and why was my heart not the way the Father of Jesus intended it to be?"

I was not looking for Christianity. Being brought up as a Catholic, I had never felt the tangible Presence of God. I had looked in other places and searched for truth in other religions to investigate God's existence, but I never found Him. I certainly did not experience what Jesus Christ had spoken of and experienced when He referred to His relationship with the Father. It was only by the grace of the Holy Spirit that my eyes were opened to the truth of the Word of God and that Jesus Christ was His Son — even if it was the only way I would ever walk again.

God showed me that His only begotten Son was Jesus Christ and that I was healed 2000 years ago when He died on the cross, shedding His blood as a ransom for all.

I was healed 2000 years ago!

9

*A*lways in life, when things go wrong or don't go exactly the way we have planned, the first thing we do is look at our life and we say that it is either our fate, our destiny, or, we blame God. When relationships don't work out, when sickness befalls us, an when an accident happens or when a loved one dies, it's only then that we mention God's name. And then, it is likely to be out of anger, frustration or shame.

This book is written for those who know the Lord Jesus and also for those who have never experienced His Presence and His word in their heart. It is written to leave the believer (or searcher) the space to go to the Lord and for the Lord to reveal Himself in their true purpose and call.

This book is in no way intended to add to, detract from or interfere with what the church is doing today. The Lord Himself will do what He will and reveal Himself to His church. This book is here to plant a seed in the heart of the believer regarding the most important prayer Jesus ever prayed, that we would 'receive' and 'realize' His promise — the promise that He died for, **AND THIS PROMISE IS WITH US NOW!**

I pray that the Lord will give me the wisdom to write all that He has given me.

~~~~~~~~

The word church means assembly.
The church is the body of Christ.

I am part of the assembly of Christ's body. The assembly means the church. And as part of this assembly, the church, my body is His body and the temple — His temple, the temple of the Holy Spirit.

This book is for all the people who feel that they cannot fit completely into a part of what today's church represents, and yet want to know where the place is. They want to be be comforted in the place of their salvation.

Is the church of today what Jesus originally intended? He wanted for us to know Him in our hearts 24 hours a day, 7 days a week. Is He satisfied with today's church, or is He looking for a new and deeper commitment? Where will this commitment start and how will it begin to grow? Is there something important that we have all missed and not seen?

This book is for those who are looking for MORE and a tearing away of the veil and a removal of the web which the establishment can lock you into.

So where do we go from here?

We must go from a place of knowing to a place of inquiring. The inquiry must come from the heart, alone. This is the place where God wins and the place He gives revelation to. It is the heart, **NOT THE MIND**.

I criticize none. Every church and ministry must judge itself. *But until Jesus is placed at the head, the Authority He left behind is only available in part.* At this moment in time in the history of the church (and her various man made sects and denominations), we are not of **ONE HEART**. Only when we have His heart can we walk in His true authority as Head. So when we talk about the place we will be comforted in our salvation, I can only describe this place as:

- The place of miracles
- The place of healing
- The place of wisdom and understanding
- The place of prosperity
- The place where you will stand in front of the gates of heaven, while still on earth
- The place of the new creation, of the inner man and where he receives the heart intended for him
- Most important of all, it is the place of **TOTAL UNITY**
- That place starts and ends in **THE HEART OF JESUS CHRIST**

"*A new heart I will give you.*"

Ezekiel 36:26

~~~~~~~~~

After going through the mill of ministry, discipleship, deliverance and even Bible Schools, there were certain areas which I wanted to change in my life but just couldn't seem to get to. Those areas revolved around the part of my Spirit that belonged to the inner man and receiving the spirit heart. I will call it the spirit heart, as it does not belong to my heart. It is immortal and just as functional as the mortal heart which pumps our blood. This heart, the spirit heart, pumps the blood of Jesus in our spirit man.

Some people read scripture and substitute the word spirit for heart, but when we look at what the Word of God says, the description of a new heart and the description of receiving the Holy Spirit are not the same. The Holy Spirit is the provider of this new heart, He is the miracle worker. Jesus said, "First, seek the Kingdom of Heaven and all things shall be added to you."

So, where is the Kingdom of Heaven?

The connection between heart and heaven is hidden in the revelation of the Word of God. As the Bible was written by the Holy Spirit, it is the promises of the Lord God the Father, sealed by **THE SHED BLOOD OF JESUS ON THE CROSS**. All we have to do is believe it and receive, walking in obedience.

To begin, we must first look at the inner man in his spirit form and see how he is built. Paul, in his letters, constantly refers to the inner man, and the Armour of God. He speaks of his protection and his mental faculties, the Spirit of wisdom and understanding, but not the construction of the inner man. There are in his letters, reference to the eyes and ears of our understanding and our feet shod in the Gospel of Peace. But no where in his teaching does he clearly define the construction of the inner man from the ground up. In fact none of the apostles talk about it clearly. It is only Peter, in his 2nd letter, when he describes the perfect and precise knowledge of Jesus Christ that we get a spark of this. Paul's letter in Ephesians (chapter 3, verses 3–18) gives us an inkling to where these great men of God have risen to in their spiritual understanding. Now, I do not dare to criticize these spiritual giants or the Word of God. I am merely stating that they have omitted this teaching. I believe they took it for granted, having received so much from the Master's Presence both in the spirit and on the earth. Perhaps they saw it as too obvious to discuss the teaching on this matter – the receiving of the new heart.

All of these letters written under the anointing of the Holy Spirit by Peter and Paul, were written as advice to the church and the early church of that time. Some of those letters were written in prisons under incredible hardships, beatings, and the threat of death itself.

We are now 2000 years down the line and what are we doing?

Jesus is risen, He is with us. His spirit is in us. What have we done?

When I started this book as the Lord led, He said to me, "Everything that I am saying in this book is backed up by the Word of God and can be revealed to anyone by the Holy Spirit, should they choose to wait on Me and ask Me." The teaching here is already revealed in the Gospels and in the letters of Peter and Paul. This book is not designed to look for shortcomings in God's Word, but rather to explore the infinite depth of God's Word and the levels of understanding within it. Our understanding of God's Word is according to how we offer up our spirits, minds and hearts to be renewed thereof.

John 14:12 says;

Most assuredly I say to you he who believes in me, the work that I do he will do also, and greater works will he do because I go to my father.

For this reason I want to discuss the quest of asking God to construct the inner man from the ground up, providing him with everything Jesus had.

When we are born again, we receive the new birth. We get baptized and the old man or old self is put down and then is raised up through the water. In baptism, we receive a circumcision of the heart. Everything is new. We receive the Holy Spirit, which makes this possible. Soon after, we find that we spend most of our time trying to break away from those who tell you what **GOD** is telling you, because you know it's not quite right.

So we begin to develop a relationship with God and the Holy Spirit, to be led by Him, but unconsciously through parts of the old man and his desires (which won't die or haven't died). We wonder how and why we can move out of God's perfect will, the place where, "We are His Workmanship (literally, His poem) created in Christ Jesus for good works which God prepared beforehand that we should walk in them" Ephesians 1:10. As the inner man is not properly formed yet in the use of his spiritual muscles, the problem is that the **OLD MAN** who has been buried, is now being dug up. This old man is prayed over for healing, but is now so fallen that he cannot listen to the Holy Spirit and follow Him in the way Jesus could. Yes, there are spiritual muscles and they grow from wisdom and understanding through the gift of faith, but the new creation still has the limits of the old heart.

The problem is that the old man, who is put down by the new creation, can only follow Jesus in part or part of the time. The part that can follow is the part that has been ministered to by others. The part which has been put under the Word of God and, in some cases, has received deliverance, by the discipline of those mentoring him. It is the old way, the unsurrendered portion of the old heart that cannot follow Christ. This dichotomy creates division in the body of Christ. It propagates growth of numbers within denominations which are aligned with different doctrines or spiritual hair splitting with the multi faceted personas and egos of man. It is time to take our hands off those who are God's. We must take our unyeilded hearts and hands off His children who were won by the blood of His Son, Jesus. We must put away our pride and self importance and let God do the mentoring. Even when it is through us, it must be God who does the mentoring by the Spirit, only then will He be the head. Only then will there be **ONE BODY, ONE HEART, ONE MIND and ONE CHURCH.**

One Body
One Heart
One Mind
One Church

For if we are to be redressed spiritually, as Jesus was originally dressed, this must only be done by God Himself. This process begins and ends with the heart as there was nowhere for Satan to land in the heart of Jesus.

So, if we are not careful to stop this mistake **NOW**, we will continue to interfere in the process Jesus has established in a person's salvation and spiritual walk. Jesus, and Jesus alone, is the Author and Finisher of our faith. We could be interfering with the destiny of God's right hand? We are in danger of placing all our limited vision as a curse on man in our blindness to see that God is more then enough. All we should be doing is helping a person to open his heart and leave him there standing before God, stripped and naked of all. At that moment, the Master Builder, the Lord Himself, can go to work and begin at the first place He finds open and enters. This is the rebuilding of the heart.

What becomes of the inner man? The inner man is waiting to take control of you but his eyes are not open, his ears are not open. He is sleeping. He is not dressed. He has no sword, and most of all, his heart has not even been started. It is allowed to function only in the natural, or in limited spiritual capacity during circumstances when the anointing is flowing.

Some Christians even try to put their heart and their own desires into the presence of the newly created inner man and his prayer life. They spend all their lives getting nowhere with God or with their call. They never fulfill their course, receive their blessings or walk into maturity. No new heart, no maturity.

In my own heart, there were areas which I could not reach with God's Word, in prayer, or even in my subconscious mind. I could not touch my dream life or the revelation to receiving what God was giving me until I realized that my inner MAN had not been built and had not received the new heart. I was paralyzed. Most of the time I was kept in a semi—conscious state, like a man in a hospital bed suffering a coma. It was then when the Lord Jesus spoke to me. He said, "Receive my heart and you will live forever."

I don't mean that if I am saved that I won't live forever — I believe in eternal life. The Lord was saying to me that I could live forever in the spiritual realm. That I could walk in and out of it, in full awareness of what I was doing and praying about. That I could feel the power of life, the power of the "spirit of the water of life" anytime I wanted. It was then, when I realized that I needed a new heart that I understood that a new heart would kill the old man completely.

That's when I asked Jesus for that new heart to be placed in my inner man. This was a covenant decision, and I desired that new heart to control everything in my walk with the Holy Spirit. It was then that I realized that my inner man was constantly being fed by God. Alcohol was an idol to me. In this covenant decision, the Father spoke to me and revealed to me, that only by giving up alcohol would I receive the new wine.

Even in the taking of the Lord's supper, I gave up wine as I am now full of the new wine. My cup overflows. No man of God can be full of the new wine constantly while being locked in idolatry in any area — especially for pastors, teachers, evangelists, prophets and apostles. Any area that is idolatry to you will keep your inner man from walking in fullness. Carnality, (such as the taking of wine or overeating or indulging in too much entertainment) contributes greatly to the "leaking out" of any new wine received. Carnality creates a spiritual barrier, keeping the believer back in his walk and further away from God.

Carnality creates a spiritual barrier, keeping the believer back in his walk and further away from God

You see, our old hearts leak. That is why we need to be constantly filled. The process of doing that yourself will only make you weary. When God gives you the new heart, He constantly fills it for you. And when you let that heart control you, you walk into different levels of vision, understanding, wisdom, power, authority, peace, joy, love, and the Kingdom of Heaven itself. This happens because we are "seated at the right hand of the Father because we are in Christ, risen with him." (Ephesians 1:20 & 2:5,10,16)

We must be ready to embrace the new life, the new heart, and ask the Lord to equip us for the changes it will bring. The Holy Spirit will witness this to you directly. If you can't hear it and you have unconfessed sin in you, are filled with carnality, or simply are unsaved, repent now for whatever it is that is troubling you with your whole heart — and see what God will say to you.

This was a difficult decision for me. For me it involved giving up alcohol and I loved my wine. I loved drinking wine, but since receiving the new wine in which you never thirst, I cannot describe the joy that overflows from the inside. I don't know what stands in your way or what it is that will be required from you. Areas that feed your flesh or draw you away from God's Presence will have to be released. It is a much better place to be in the Presence of the Lord than to walk in the lust of the flesh. What more is there? He is more than enough. (Ezekiel 36:25-30)

~~~~~~~~~~~~~~~~~~~

*"A new heart
I will give you."*
Ezekiel 36:26

~~~~~~~~~~~~~~~~~~~

Chapter 1

~~~~~~~~~~

The Kingdom
of the Heart

Melchizedek king of Salem [later called Jerusalem] brought out bread and wine [for their nourishment]; he was the priest of God Most High, And he blessed him and said, Blessed (favored with blessings, made blissful, joyful) be Abram by God Most High, Possessor and Maker of heaven and earth, and blessed, praised, and glorified be God Most High, Who has given your foes into your hand! And [Abram] gave him a tenth of all [he had taken]. Gen 14:18–20 AMP

The Lord has sworn and will not revoke or change it: You are a priest forever, after the manner and order of Melchizedek. Ps 110:4 AMP

> *Where Jesus has entered in for us [in advance], a Forerunner having become a High Priest forever after the order (with the rank) of Melchizedek. Heb 6:20 AMP*

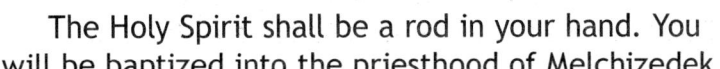

The Holy Spirit shall be a rod in your hand. You will be baptized into the priesthood of Melchizedek.

Melchizidek was a Prototype of Christ

The rod is always used to subdue. Even though we can receive a new heart, we will always need to stand on the Word of God and subdue our flesh. With a new heart this is so much easier. Only with Christ can you walk in total fulfilment of your purpose and destiny. Jesus is ALWAYS there for you — ready to be your personal Saviour.

As a result of a severe automobile accident, there was great injury to my back. The doctor told me that the S1, S2, and S3 disks had been squeezed out like tooth paste. The force of the impact to my lower back had also moved part of my spine completely out of alignment. Following an MRI scan, I was told I would never be able to walk without crutches, and that I would have only limited use of my right leg.

As a solution, I was prescribed various painkillers which did little to help. With great determination, I tried several alternative means of healing myself. I would hang upside down for hours lifting weights while in this reversed position. I tried massage therapy and chiropractic treatments. None of these things worked.

At best, they brought about temporary relief from the pain, but never increased my mobility. In fact, I would usually experience about a 50 to 60 % relief from pain that would last for only about 20 minutes at a time. It was completely frustrating. Everything felt beyond my control and I was helpless to make the situation better.

Even just being in a car was incredibly painful. Just breathing in would cause spasms of pain. It came to the point where there was so much activity in the nervous system of my spine that I could not even keep food down. I suffered vomiting fits and terrible side effects that made my life a living misery.

I had been living with this injury for a long time and the damage to my spine was getting worse. There was nothing holding my spine straight at its base. It wasn't until I met somebody who was filled with the Holy Spirit who told me that Jesus Christ was a real alternative to what I was living with that I ever considered the possibility of believing for something better — for healing! This woman told me that Jesus Christ was a healer and that everything He said was the truth. It was astonishing. It filled me with hope and I dared to believe.

It was astonishing, it filled me with hope and I dared to believe

Now, I am not saying that this is an easy choice for anyone to make. It is radical and no matter how desperate we are, surrendering total trust and submitting our lives in order to believe in Jesus is not easy. But, let's consider this; God sent his only son to die on a cross for you.

Now whether you can accept this or not, whether you choose to believe this or not, that sacrifice was made for you. The promise of eternal life (and a complete life) was put in place for you. Accepting Christ and receiving salvation makes you whole. The sacrifice of Jesus was made so that you would be set free from three curses.

The Curse of Poverty: Unrestrained lack upon the majority of humanity.

The Curse of Sickness: The release of physical corruption and decay.

The Curse of 2nd Death: The reality of spiritual death beyond physical death.

These are curses that have been released as a result of the fall of Adam. Because of Adam's fall, we are born with a sin nature. Thus, we are subject to these curses without our choosing. Jesus Christ is the only path to freedom from these afflictions. You can be set free from poverty, sickness and death!

For me, the moment that I opened my heart to receive the broken body of Jesus on that cross – the instant that I recognized the price He paid for me – barely grasping the suffering that He overcame and the abuse he endured as a perfect sacrifice for me – that was the moment I went back 2,000 years to the foot of that cross, and I mean I was standing in front of it, and it was then that I gave my heart to Jesus. When I considered the magnitude of His sacrifice for my life and wholeness, I felt small. But when I considered the scope of His mercy and unconditional love, I was overwhelmed. He had captivated me and in that moment, surrendering to His great love was the most natural thing I had ever done.

I prayed these words, "God, come in into my heart. Jesus, I love you. I know that You are my Saviour and the Son of God — the true Christ. Save me, heal me, take all of me. In return I give you my life to do with as you will. I want to be of service to you and for your glory. I give myself completely to you and to our Father with whom I am reconciled with in your Name. Come and live inside me. I want everything you have to give. Holy Sprit, enter me now, fill me; I receive my healing now — right now! Amen."

There, in that instant, I made the decision for my heart to change. Now, this is not the heart I am speaking of in this book, but it was the doorway of the beginning.

The Miracle

What does it mean to receive a miracle? I want to explain to you as best I can what it is like to receive a miracle from God.

After I opened my heart to the Lord Jesus, it began. Now if you asked me what I was doing, I would have to say that I was doing nothing. The Bible tells us that each man has received a portion of faith.

> *For through the grace given to me I say to every man among you not to think more highly of himself than he ought to think; but to think so as to have sound judgment, as God has allotted to each a measure of faith. Romans 12:3 NASB*

I am not talking about the ordinary measure of faith that we have been given in order to receive hope. Neither am I speaking of the faith needed to grasp the substance of things that we believe into our spirits. "And whatever you ask for in prayer,

having faith and [really] believing, you will receive."
Matthew 21:22 AMP "And He said to her, Daughter,
your faith (your trust and confidence in Me, springing
from faith in God) has restored you to health. Go in
(into) peace and be continually healed and freed from
your [distressing bodily] disease" Mark 5:34 AMP.

I am talking about a special gift of faith – one of
the power gifts of the Holy Spirit. This gift is WHEN
YOU DO NOTHING AND GOD DOES EVERYTHING.

> *What if some did not believe and were*
> *without faith? Do their lack of faith and their*
> *faithlessness nullify and make ineffective and*
> *void the faithfulness of God and His fidelity*
> *[to His Word]?* **By no means! Let God be**
> **found true though every human being is**
> **false and a liar,** *as it is written, That You*
> *may be justified and shown to be upright*
> *in what You say, and prevail when You are*
> *judged [by sinful men]. Romans 3:3–4 AMP*

My spine felt like someone had crushed it. It was
smashed together like an accordion's bellows after all
the air has been pressed out. Then, I felt the right hand
of God reach inside my body and grip my spine. Before I
had ever even spoken the first word of the prayer to ask
God for my healing — healing had begun. I started to
speak in tongues. Something dark was pushed out of my
body as the Holy Spirit entered me and gave me power.

As this continued, my spine — every single
vertebrae and disk — started to "POP" open. There
was a literal, audible popping sound which could
be heard in the room. My spine was popping open.
God had healed my spine, and filled me as I was
experiencing all this happening to me. The Holy

Spirit began moving my mouth. I looked into a mirror and God had taken 10 years of my face. The pain had gone. I could stand. I could walk. I could run. I could even lift weights. My strength returned to me as strong and enduring as when I was a teenager. I was renewed, revived! I had experienced revival of the mind and Spirit. I had accepted God's priceless gift of salvation and I had been healed.

Straight from the Word

I want to share some Scripture with you. I want you to understand the measure of what you possess in Him.

"Blessed be the God and Father of our Lord Jesus Christ, who has blessed us with every spiritual blessing in the heavenly places in Christ..." Ephesians 1: 3 NKJV

There is more to this scripture than we are experiencing today. This verse tells us that we have everything that the Father blessed Jesus with! Get that — can you get that? Can you stand on it? We don't need someone else to bless us. We don't need someone else to protect us. The Father, Who created everything in the whole Universe, Who created time itself, and Who always was, is going to bless us in the heavenly places in Christ. Now, let's read on:

"...just as He chose us in Him before the foundation of the world, that we should be holy and without blame before Him in love..." Ephesians 1: 4 NKJV

He chose us, you see. It was His desire for us, His

love for us that caused Him to sacrifice Himself for us and provide adoption for us into His own family.

> *"...having predestined us to adoption as sons by Jesus Christ to Himself, according to the good pleasure of His will..." Ephesians 1: 5 NKJV*

We are adopted as sons by Jesus Christ.

> *"...to the praise of the glory of His grace, by which He made us accepted in the Beloved." Ephesians 1:6 NKJV*

The Beloved is the body of Christ – it is union with Jesus.

> *"In Him we have redemption through His blood, the forgiveness of sins, according to the riches of His grace 8 which He made to abound toward us in all wisdom and prudence, 9 having made known to us the mystery of His will, according to His good pleasure which He purposed in Himself..." Ephesians 1:7–9 NKJV*

We have been transferred from the kingdom of darkness to the Kingdom of God. When a slave's redemption was purchased — he was made a free man. Jesus has purchased our redemption for us with the price of His own blood. He has forgiven our sins and extended His grace to us. He opens the door for our destiny and the ability to walk confidently in His will. Even better, we learn that this is His pleasure — it delights Him to provide this great gift to us!

> *"...that in the dispensation of the fullness of the times He might gather together in one all things*

*in Christ, both which are in heaven and which
are on earth — in Him. Ephesians 1: 9—10 NKJV*

Another translation says it this way:

*"...a long-range plan in which everything
would be brought together and summed
up in Him, everything in deepest heaven,
everything on planet earth." Ephesians 1:9—10*
(From THE MESSAGE: The Bible in Contemporary Language
© 2002 by Eugene H. Peterson. All rights reserved.)

We are to walk in the fullness of the times. We
recognize the scope of past, present and future
tenses of victory. God's plan covers it all!

*"He has delivered us from the power of darkness
and conveyed us into the Kingdom of the Son
of His love, 14 in whom we have redemption
through His blood, the forgiveness of sins. 15 He
is the image of the invisible God, the firstborn
over all creation." Colossians 1:13—15 NKJV*

These verses also speak of the transfer from the
kingdom (power/authority) of darkness into the Kingdom
(power/authority) of the Son. It again confirms our
redemption. Even more exciting to me is what follows;

*"...**HAVING WIPED OUT THE HANDWRITING
OF REQUIREMENTS THAT WAS AGAINST
US,** which was contrary to us. And He has
taken it out of the way, **HAVING NAILED
IT TO THE CROSS**. 15 Having disarmed
principalities and powers, **HE MADE A PUBLIC
SPECTACLE OF THEM TRIUMPHING OVER
THEM, IN IT."** Colossians 2:14 — 15 NKJV*

Another translation puts it like this;

"When you were stuck in your old sin—dead

*life, you were incapable of responding to God. God brought you alive — right along with Christ! Think of it! All sins forgiven, **THE SLATE WIPED CLEAN**, that old arrest warrant cancelled and **NAILED TO CHRIST'S CROSS. HE STRIPPED ALL THE SPIRITUAL TYRANTS IN THE UNIVERSE OF THEIR SHAM AUTHORITY AT THE CROSS AND MARCHED THEM NAKED THROUGH THE STREETS.** Colossians 2:13—15*

(From THE MESSAGE: The Bible in Contemporary Language © 2002 by Eugene H. Peterson. All rights reserved.)

Jesus wiped out all of our sins and wiped the slate clean by nailing them to the cross once and for all. He disarmed the devil himself and all his principalities and powers. He put them in chains and paraded them publicly in the heavenlies, making them a display for eternity.

Eph 2:7 tells us

"THAT IN THE AGES TO COME HE MIGHT SHOW THE EXEEDING RICHES OF HIS GRACE IN HIS KINDNESS TOWARDS US IN CHRIST JESUS." NKJV

It goes on to say in Eph 2:10

"FOR WE ARE HIS WORKMANSHIP, CREATED IN JESUS CHRIST FOR GOOD WORKS WHICH GOD PREPARED BEFORE HAND THAT WE SHOULD WALK IN THEM." NKJV

The literal translation of the word "workmanship" is "poem" — we are God's poem, created in Christ Jesus for good works. Created to walk in good works. So how do we walk in them?

Look at what Jesus said in Revelation 3:20.

*"Behold I stand at the door and knock, if
anyone hears my voice and opens the door
I will come in to him and will eat with
him and he will eat with me." AMP*

My wife once shared with me a revelation that
she had received from the Lord. He said to her,
"When you don't pray with your whole heart to me
you don't pray to me. There are many others gods."

I must say that this disturbed me. Was I really praying
with my whole heart? But then, I looked at revelation
3: 20 again. If Jesus is standing at the door and the
door is my heart, then He can come in and He can take
the knowledge of my heart. Jesus said that the Father
knows what is in your heart, even before you ask for
it in prayer. Jesus and the Father know your heart.

**So then, I asked myself, "If we are blessed with
every spiritual blessing in the heavenly places in
Christ, why can't I be
blessed and receive the
heart of Jesus? Then
I can always pray to
God with a whole heart
just as Jesus did."**

*Why can't I
be blessed and
receive the
heart of Jesus?*

To receive the heart of
Jesus is an awesome blessing
for the inner man. It is what
God originally intended for the revived, renewed, born
again man. I want to look at the place of receiving,
but first, let's look at the point of being blessed.

Let's say that a man comes up to you in the street
and says to you: "I am going to bless you with 1,000 tons

of gold. I am going to bless you with three airplanes, and I am going to bless you with ten cars..." Okay, stop right there, lets look at the first blessing, the gold.

You ask yourself, "How am I going to move all that gold? What am I going to do with the gold once it is moved? How will I keep it safe?"

And then, you begin to wonder about the other gifts, "How am I going to get those three airplanes in the second blessing — I don't even know how to fly! Where I can use them and for what? And, what am I going to do with the ten cars in the third blessing?"

"I might need a train to move the gold. I will need three pilots and maybe three co-pilots to move the planes and somewhere to park them. I might need a driving license and\or drivers to move the cars, and once they are moved, where will they be kept? Who will pay the insurance? What will we use them for?"

The focus is all wrong. The man intends the gifts to bless you so you can be a blessing to others. He has considered the logistics and has a plan in place — but you are fretting and unsure and are likely to pass the blessing by because you cannot get a handle on all of the details.

We are talking about the equipping of the heart in the areas of every spiritual blessing pertaining to God's purpose in his predestined will in us. Can you get that into your Spirit? What a blessing the Father is to us. Where would we be without Him? Without him, we are dust, that's all I can say — and so does the word.

Let's pray this scripture (Ezekiel 36: 25–29), together and receive the blessings of the new heart. Let's ask the Lord to equip the new heart He is going to give us to be able to receive every spiritual blessing in Christ Jesus.

Ezekiel 36: 25-29

25 "Then I will sprinkle clean water upon you and you shall be clean from all your uncleanness and from all idols (the self and its vain imaginations we are to cast down, the created image and other gods) will I cleanse you.

God - I receive this cleansing.

26 "A NEW HEART WILL I GIVE YOU AND A NEW SPIRIT, (a new quest and divine personality) WILL I PUT WITHIN YOU AND I WILL PUT AWAY, THE STONY HEART OUT OF YOUR FLESH AND GIVE YOU A HEART OF FLESH.

God, give me this new heart and new spirit. Give me a heart of flesh for my heart of stone.

27 "And I will put My spirit within you and cause you to walk in My statues and you shall heed My ordinances, (creations) and do them.

God, I receive Your spirit. I desire to walk in your statutes and fulfill my purpose.

28 "And you shall dwell in the land that I gave to your fathers and you shall be My people and I will be your God.

God, I desire to dwell in the land and be yours.

29 "I WILL SAVE YOU, from all your uncleanness AND I WILL CALL FORTH THE GRAIN (provision) and make it abundant and lay no famine on you.

God, thank you for saving me from unrighteousness. I embrace your abundant provision and rejoice in your protection.

30 "And I will multiply the fruit of the tree and the increase of the field that you may no more suffer the reproach and disgrace of famine among the Nations."

God, thank you for harvest and increase. Thank you for lifting me above reproach and disgrace and blessing me among the Nations.

Chapter 2

The Change of Heart

The Receiving of a New Heart

When Christ died for us in order to purchase our redemption, He did not purchase us in part, or only a small piece. He purchased us in full — our total self. Because of this, He desires that we walk in wholeness of mind, spirit, soul and body.

When we accept Him as our Saviour, He becomes the King and we, the loyal subject. It is only natural for us to assert our rights and try to dictate our own path. Submission is difficult. Christ has become King of our heart by purchase. However, ONLY when we receive this new heart - when we allow God to replace our heart of stone for a new heart of flesh, does He become King of our lives by a gracious and willing coronation. Submission is difficult — surrender is sweet.

In the book of Ezekiel, the promise of a new heart is recorded.

> *I will give you a* **new heart** *and put a* **new**
> **spirit** *within you; I will take the heart*
> *of stone out of your flesh and give you*
> *a heart of flesh. Ezekiel 36:26 NKJV*

The Lord is talking about a new heart **and** a new spirit. This new heart and new spirit are not the same thing. They are not an interchangeable reality — they are two different things.

New Heart

This heart is fixed upon Jesus and firmly resolved to follow Christ in all things.

God said that He would give his people a new heart. A heart that is whole. A heart this is single and allied only with the true God. It is no longer divided among many gods (idols). This heart is fixed upon Jesus and firmly resolved to follow Christ in all things. It is a steady heart. It is a heart that is not wavering with doubt or unbelief or distraction. This heart is sincere.

New Spirit

God also promised that He would put a new spirit in you. Having a new name or a new face is of no value unless there is a new spirit living inside you. This spirit must be in union with the One who created you. This spirit is in agreement with the voice of God and is in tune with the desires of God. The Bible says that if any man be in Christ, he is a new creature. This new creature is given a new spirit.

> *Then I will give them one heart, and I will put a new spirit within them, and take the stony heart out of their flesh, and give them a heart of flesh, that they may walk in My statutes and keep My judgments and do them; and they shall be My people, and I will be their God. Ezekiel 11:19–20 NKJV*

Stony Heart

God says he will take the stony heart out of you. This stony heart is dead, spiritually. It is dry and hardened. It does not bear fruit — it is like stone.

Heart of Flesh

In place of the stony heart, God puts in a new heart of flesh. This heart is alive spiritually. This new heart is sensitive and tender. This is God's gift to you. It is a wonderful experience to journey from dead works into life abundant!

~~~~~~~~~~

HAVE YOU RECEIVED THIS HEART?

DO YOU HAVE THE
LORD'S HEART WITHIN YOU?

~~~~~~~~~~

Chapter 3

The Visitation

It was midnight. My wife had gone out with her family. I was alone and had begun to seek the Lord regarding the issue of the New Heart. All of the sudden, I had a powerful visitation with the Lord Jesus. He appeared in front of me and said, "Do not take the eyes of your heart from me, and then you will fear no evil."

As I looked at His face, I could see for the first time that my heart was coming alive. I recognized that it had been dead before and was beginning to burst forth with life. The feeling was indescribable. The love I had for the Lord was uncontainable. It was as if all boundaries and barriers had been lifted from me and I was able to reach beyond my human capacity to love and experience a supernatural ability to love. The sin that once attacked parts of my mind was burned away. I began to cry. Tenderly, I looked into His eyes — the eyes of the One who redeemed me and I saw the place where my salvation was won.

It was excruciating. The pain I witnessed in Him was more than I could bear to look upon. It convicted my every thought. Then, as I continued in His Presence, Jesus said to me, "Come with me. Come."

Something opened before me and we were standing in a room inside a fortress on the top of a mountain. Behind Him, I could see through the windows and take in the landscape and the sky. When I turned around, I realized that the room we were in was vast. We walked to a corner and the Lord opened a drawer. There was a wall filled with drawers. The drawer He opened was small, and as he pulled it open He took out a small box. He opened the box and revealed a ring.

The ring had three black stones in it. The stones were so black that they were like holes in the space we were in. Then the Lord spoke to me and said, "This was your ring, now it is mine. Put it away."

He could see my every thought and answered my question before I spoke

He could see my every thought and answered my question before I spoke.

"The ring," He said, "is the old covenant that you had with the world. The three stones in the ring represent blindness to the Father, blindness to the Son and blindness to the Holy Spirit."

I caught a glimpse of the past when the ring was on my finger. I saw that it had grown veins to my heart, to my head, to my soul and even to my body. This caused stubborness, stress, heart disease, cancer and death.

"You gave Me the right to remove this ring from you when you gave Me your life," He said.

Then I looked at my hand and saw a golden band on my ring finger. "Now you are a part of My bride," He began, "Only those who give me their whole heart can become My bride, and theirs is the Kingdom of Heaven. For when the heart belongs to Me, it becomes eternal, just as all that I say and all that I am is eternal, as is My Father in Heaven is eternal. When your heart is eternal it becomes infinite. It is ready for the fire that comes from My presence."

There was a pause as this began to sink in to my spirit. Then, He said, "Walk with me a while, I have much to show you." And we began to walk together.

"Tell them," He continued, "That they must exchange their hearts from mortal to immortal. The words I give are miracles — for they are filled with My presence. But in order to receive the power of My words, they need new hearts."

At that point the Lord began to cry. I saw tears form and begin to well up in His eyes. As thoughts began to flood my mind..."How is it possible for me to give this message,"...He vanished.

Without faith, we cannot see God. But He left for me a key. That key to His presence is the place where I want to lead you. It is my earnest desire that through my testimony you too will begin to walk in a new relationship with Him. Jesus died for you more than 2000 years ago at place called Golgotha. He was alone, beaten and torn to pieces, cursed and covered in bruises, cuts and His own blood. He was denied a trial and was nailed to a cross even though He was without sin. The Lamb of God. A perfect Lamb without blemish was led to slaughter as a ransom for many. As a ransom for you.

I invite you to pray this prayer now.

Prayer for a New Heart

~~~~~~~~~~

My Lord Jesus, equip my heart for this change. I cut out my old heart and give it to You. Return your heart to me. Give me the immortal, the infinite that was made in Your sacred image. God, open the eyes of that heart. Open the ears and the mouth so that I may now learn and enter new life.

~~~~~~~~~~

Chapter 4

~~~~~~~~~~~

The Fountain of Man's Deeds.

As I meditated and studied the heart, I used Strong's Concordance and Vine's Concise Dictionary of the Bible. These works have a great deal to offer on the heart, and I want to share with you some of the insights I gained while studying.

The heart is regarded as the seat of emotions. It is characterized as the hidden springs of personal life, for joy or for fear and sorrows. This hidden quality, the ability to keep things veiled from others is what makes it so necessary for a heart to be pure in order to stand in the presence of God.

The heart is:

- The seat of physical life
- The seat of emotions and passions
- The seat of consciousness
- The seat of appetites
- The seat of courage
- The hidden springs of personal life
- The fountain of man's deeds
- The seat of grief
- The inner man

The heart of man has a personality, is the centre of moral character, is capable of making decisions and, most importantly, is the place where man responds to God.

> *You shall love the LORD your God with all your heart, with all your soul, and with all your strength. Deut 6:5 NKJV*

The heart is the fountain of man's deeds.

> *Then Hezekiah turned his face toward the wall, and prayed to the LORD, and said, "Remember now, O LORD, I pray, how I have walked before You in truth and with a loyal heart, and have done what is good in Your sight" Isaiah 38:2–3 NKJV.*

A pure heart can stand in God's presence.

*Who may ascend into the hill of the LORD? Or
who may stand in His holy place? He who has
clean hands and a pure heart, Who has not lifted
up his soul to an idol, nor sworn deceitfully.
He shall receive blessing from the LORD, And
righteousness from the God of his salvation.*

Psalm 24:3–5 NKJV

Because of the natural heart — unredeemed and divided — man's only hope is the promise of God.

*Then I will sprinkle clean water on you, and you
shall be clean; I will cleanse you from all your
filthiness and from all your idols. I will give you
a new heart and put a new spirit within you; I
will take the heart of stone out of your flesh and
give you a heart of flesh. Ezekiel 36:25–26 NKJV*

The heart can be cleaned.

*Create in me a clean heart, O God, And renew
a steadfast spirit within me. Psalm 51:10 NKJV*

The heart can be tested.

*Search me, O God, and know my heart: try
me, and know my thoughts;And see if there
be any wicked way in me, and lead me in
the way everlasting. Psalm 139: 23–24 ASV*

I, the LORD, search the heart, I test the mind, Even to give every man according to his ways, According to the fruit of his doings.

Jeremiah 17:10 NKJV

The heart can escape man's understanding. We need God's intervention.

Who can understand his errors? Cleanse me from secret faults. Keep back Your servant also from presumptuous sins; Let them not have dominion over me. Then I shall be blameless, And I shall be innocent of great transgression. Let the words of my mouth and the meditation of my heart Be acceptable in Your sight, O LORD, my strength and my Redeemer.

Psalm 19: 12–14 NKJV

The heart can become hard.

But encourage one another daily, as long as it is called Today, so that none of you may be hardened by sin's deceitfulness. We have come to share in Christ if we hold firmly till the end the confidence we had at first. As has just been said: "Today, if you hear his voice, do not harden your hearts as you did in the rebellion." Hebrews 3:13–15 NIV

At the last, the heart bites like a serpent and stings like a viper.

Your eyes will see strange things, And your heart will utter perverse things.

Yes, you will be like one who lies down in the midst of the sea, Or like one who lies at the top of the mast, saying: "They have struck me, but I was not hurt; They have beaten me, but I did not feel it..."

Proverbs 23:32—35 NKJV

The word heart comes from the word *leb* which in Hebrew means, the inner man, the mind, the will, the heart, understanding the inner part, the midst. *Leb* is a synonym of *lebab* which often means the inner person, with a focus on the physical aspects of the mind and heart[1], which also includes doing the will of God from the heart — this becomes the seat of faith.

Teach me Your way, O LORD; I will walk in Your truth; Unite my heart to fear Your name. I will praise You, O Lord my God, with all my heart, And I will glorify Your name forevermore.

Psalm 86:11 NKJV

Create in me a clean heart, O God, And renew a steadfast spirit within me. Do not cast me away from Your presence, And do not take Your Holy Spirit from me. Restore to me the joy of Your salvation, And uphold me by Your

[1]*The Online Bible Thayer's Greek Lexicon and Brown Driver & Briggs Hebrew Lexicon, Copyright © 1993, Woodside Bible Fellowship, Ontario, Canada. Licensed from the Institute for Creation Research.)*

generous Spirit. Then I will teach transgressors Your ways, And sinners shall be converted to You. Deliver me from the guilt of bloodshed, O God, the God of my salvation, And my tongue shall sing aloud of Your righteousness. O Lord, open my lips, And my mouth shall show forth Your praise. For You do not desire sacrifice, or else I would give it; You do not delight in burnt offering. The sacrifices of God are a broken spirit, A broken and a contrite heart — These, O God, You will not despise.

Psalm 51: 10–17 NKJV

Jesus said that you cannot put new wine into old wine skins, or the old skins would burst. He also said that you cannot sew a new piece of cloth onto an old garment, or the garment would tear.

What is the heart?

Physically, the heart is the body's pump, cycling life—giving blood to the vital organs. Let's look at this in spiritual significance. Spiritually, the heart is the place of reasoning powers, the place of understanding and the WILL. The heart is the centre of life and the life of the soul, (imagination, emotion and intellect), is in the heart.

When our bodies are the temple of the Holy Spirit, Jesus is the head and we have the heart of Jesus pumping His blood - His life—giving blood through every part of us.

In Ephesians 1:22–23, Paul said, "And He put all things under His feet, and gave Him to be head over all things to the church (assemblies, temples — as in your own body), which is His body, the fullness of Him who fills all in all" NKJV.

So Jesus is head over (against), sickness, disease and all evil. The failure of the church is because Jesus is wholly dependent on the body, as the head is wholly dependent on the body.

The Lord has been hindered because his body has failed to respond. His body does not know how to behave as it is seated at the right hand of the Father. When we receive the heart of Jesus (the heart being the seat of emotions and that seat being placed in heavenly places — Ephesians 1:20), doing the will of God from the heart becomes the power seat of faith. This gives a whole new meaning to the word faith. You see, we have been taught that faith is the substance of things hoped for. If we leave it at just that, then this is indeed a limiting statement. This limitation places a seed of doubt in us. Hope is not solid enough to stand under the trials before us. God wants us to remove the limitations and give life to this statement. He wants us to go forward with HIM.

When we receive the HEART OF JESUS, there are no trials before us. Our heart is dead, and therefore, the trials before us are dead. Jesus won all His victories, so we just walk in victory with him. As in the word of God, when we walk in life, only in the footsteps of GOD can we proceed.

There are two points which we must cross and God's promise is that we can cross these two points. It requires that we walk across by faith. Only when we have put our foot down in mid air, is the path is revealed. Faith is the vehicle which will open our spiritual eyes, and not just to hope, but to the promises of God that Jesus died for. Faith shows us the truth that, only when he was resurrected from the dead, could we understand, that our eyes were opened and that we could see for the first time since the fall of man.

Just as "we cannot put new wine into old wine skins, lest they break and the wine be lost," or that we "cannot put a new piece of cloth on a old garment," there must be a complete sweeping away of the old, in order to receive the new. The heart of Jesus is a fountain of life — fed from Life itself, which springs from the Water of Life which fed the Tree of Life in the Garden of Eden.

> *If anyone is thirsty, let him come to me and drink. Whoever believes in me, as the Scripture has said, streams of living water will flow from within him."*
>
> *John 7: 37b - 38a NIV*
>
> *For the wages of sin is death, but the gift of God is eternal life in Christ Jesus our Lord.*
>
> *Romans 6:23 NIV*
>
> *But the Counselor, the Holy Spirit, whom the Father will send in my name, will teach you all things and will remind you of everything I have said to you.*
>
> *John 14:26 NIV*
>
> *...I will open my mouth in parables; I will utter things hidden from the foundation of the world.*
>
> *Matthew 13:35 ASV*

There, in Matthew 13:35, you have the essence of all that there was before the foundation of the world, before Eden was ever created. The heart of Jesus holds these secrets and He has promised to reveal these hidden things to us.

The Greek word **sklerokardia**, means hardness of heart. **Sklero** (hardened) and **kardia** (heart). **Kardiagnosis** means a knower of hearts. **Kardia** (heart) **gnosis** (to know).

> *Then they prayed, "Lord, you know everyone's heart...*
>
> *Acts 1:24a NIV*

Looking at the Heart of Man

The heart of man represents the true character of man, but conceals it. It has an identity which is an enigma to understand. And yet, from the heart comes our ability to make decisions. It is the seat of grief, the seat of our moral nature and of our spiritual life. God tries the heart, He tests the heart. God cleanses the heart, guards the heart, and when you let Him rule the heart, He turns it and purifies it. The old heart we have is an enigma which keeps us balancing on the questions of free will. Yet, the heart is a kingdom so vast, that we fear to enter it in this earthly form. Until we die, we cannot see it clearly. The flesh is the bridge which allows the substance of it. The flesh, in its fallen state, always seeks to confuse the identity of the heart that God originally intended for us to have. Therefore, we are part blind in this earthly state. Only Jesus can really see eternal things.

> *So we fix our eyes not on what is seen,*
> *but on what is unseen. For what is seen is*
> *temporary, but what is unseen is eternal.*
>
> *2 Corinthians 4:18 NIV*

In order to be humble, God gives grace through the love of the Spirit. Grace is the voice of the Holy Spirit and it can be heard in the heart. The gates of the heart's kingdom of our old heart is where Jesus stands and says, "Behold I stand at the door and knock."

God's inspiration brings about voluntary assent. Once we have walked into the Kingdom, we can stand at the foot of the mountain and only then can GOD SHOW US WHAT IS TO BE BELIEVED.

Conquering the Flesh

We must starve the worldly appetite of the soul. The old nature must be conformed to the consciousness of Christ. We can only conquer the flesh by walking into the Kingdom of Heaven through it's gates as Jesus said in Matthew 13:46, "The kingdom of heaven is like a man who is a dealer in search of fine and precious pearls, who, on finding a single pearl of great price, went and sold all he had to posses it."

To conquer the old nature, we must give our whole heart to the Lord.

To conquer the old nature, we must give our whole heart to the Lord. We don't apply the Holy Spirit to our flesh, we apply the Holy Spirit to our heart. Our flesh comes under submission to our heart — our decision maker, our moral centre.

Only when the heart is totally submitted to Christ will the flesh yield in submission to it. This is why it is so important for us to define the heart in all that we do, think, say and remember in our mind's eye. We do this until we respond to every challenge with the Holy Spirit and the Holy Spirit ALONE.

I have listed below an expansion of the descriptions of the heart.

The Natural Heart

- *VITAL ORGAN THAT PUMPS BLOOD, ALLOWING THE BODY TO SUSTAIN LIFE*

The Nature of the Heart

- *"LEB" / HEART / MIND (LEBAB, INNER PERSON)*
- *THE PART OF MAN WHICH THINKS*
- *HAS A PERSONALITY AND RESPONDS TO GOD*
- *IS KNOWN ALSO AS THE INNER PART OR MIDDLE OF A SPACE*
- *IT CAN DEFINE THE WHOLE CIRCUIT OF ITS ACTION*
- *THE SEAT OF EMOTIONS — FOR JOY OR FEAR OR SORROW*
- *THE SEAT OF CONSCIOUSNESS*
- *THE SEAT OF CONSCIENCE*
- *THE SEAT OF MORAL CHARACTER*
- *THE HOPE OF IT (THE HEART) IS IN THE PROMISE OF GOD*
- *THE HEART CAN BE TESTED*
- *THE HEART CAN BE CLEANED*
- *THE HEART CAN BECOME HARDENED*

And yet, with all these qualities, even with the heart being the very centre of a man's emotional and spiritual being, it is still possible that a man still cannot understand his own heart. Parts of the heart are hidden from him — hidden from all but God. Only a pure heart is able to stand in God's presence (Psalm 24:3–4). The only way a heart can be pure is if it is submitted totally to Christ. Only through the righteousness of Christ is our heart ever pure enough to stand before God. It is His gift to us.

Going forward with God

Ray McCully, from Rhema Church in South Africa was preaching. He was talking about going forward with God and the law of motion. That in order for something to move forward, something must first be added to it. He said, "Put something into motion to go forward with God." This brings us back to receiving Jesus' heart. Receiving His heart puts something in motion. This allows us to go forward with God.

St. Augustine says, "The responsibility for evil and sin is to be found in the human will and nowhere else, just as the reason for anything good is to be found in the divine will of God and nowhere else."

The Bible describes human depravity as being rooted in the heart. "For out of the heart come evil thoughts, murder, adultery, sexual immorality, theft, false testimony, slander" Matthew 15:19 NIV. Sin is a principality, which has its seat in the centre of man's inward life and then defiles the whole circuit of his action. Scripture also describes the heart as the sphere of divine influence, (Romans 2:14–15) and that lying deep within the heart is the hidden man

— the real man (1 Peter 3:4). The heart represents the true character of a man, but conceals it.[2]

So, does this mean that we cannot know our true self? Is our heart to remain hidden from us? Jesus said, "Then you will know the truth, and the truth will set you free" John 8:32 NIV. The real you is full of truth — which is the Word filling your being inside the hidden man. Your will must be conformed to God's image. "And be not conformed to this world: but be ye transformed by the renewing of your mind, that ye may prove what is that good, and acceptable, and perfect, will of God" Romans 12:2. This can only be done when we yield to the Holy Spirit in the heart. Truth is a person — it is Jesus. Truth sets us free. Accepting this, knowing this — requires the evidence of faith in order to be believed and this truth (Jesus) can only be received without question or doubt. This is only possible in the heart — we are not capable of this in our mind. This must occur in "the hidden person of the heart, with the incorruptible beauty (the beauty being Christ) of a gentle and quiet spirit, which is (present tense) very precious in the sight of God" 1 Peter 3:4 NKJV.

The heart is the place where we receive salvation. Only when the will is broken and our emotion is moved to Christ's heart (and begins to be conformed to Him — even if only in part), is a person saved. This salvation is the love of Christ beyond the self. This decision of the heart is the key point of entry into the divine will of God.

---

2 From *Vine's Expository Dictionary of Biblical Words*, © 1985, *Thomas Nelson Publishers.*

He made you Alive

And you He made alive, who were dead in trespasses and sins.

Ephesians 2:1 NKJV

When Jesus died on the cross, all sin was forgiven... even yours!

Heaven's Gateway

I believe there is a Gateway to Heaven that men can have access to when we are in deep prayer and/or when we encounter a profound or endure a formidable experience. In those moments, a person may receive the keys to open the door to the road to Heaven's Gateway. The entrance is guarded by two angels, one on each side, who only let in those on earth who are alive and who have been given permission to enter. I believe that these two angels are the same two angels that cast man out of the Garden of Eden all those years ago!

Those who enter are either in a state of dream, in sudden temporal death, in a coma, or in deep communion with God. They are known by their hearts (Matthew 6:7–8), and trusted of God to enter. I believe that the dimension of the heart's will is the place where this permission is granted. I also believe that as the heart is the "seat of emotion" — the Gateway to Heaven is experienced here.

The Fruit of the Spirit

Before we can enter into this land where the Kingdom of God begins, we must first look at the fruit of the Holy Spirit concerning the areas of the heart.

But the fruit of the Spirit is love, joy, peace, longsuffering, kindness, goodness, faithfulness, gentleness, self—control. Against such there is no law. And those who are Christ's have crucified the flesh with its passions and desires. If we live in the Spirit, let us also walk in the Spirit. Galatians 5:22—25 NKJV

In this scripture LOVE is listed first. Then joy, peace, long suffering, kindness, goodness, faithfulness, gentleness, and finally self control. Here is the key — LOVE. We must live and walk in the Spirit with that LOVE.

We must guard our heart, lest it wax cold. It is important to remain tender in our heart, for the tender hearted receive the Word of the Lord. If you heart is hard, you will not hear Him speak.

In the book of Matthew, Chapter 13, Jesus is telling the parable of the sower. As He finishes the parable in verse 23 He says, "But he who received seed on the good ground is he who hears the word and understands it who indeed bears fruit and produces some 30, some 60 and some 100 fold." Jesus continues speaking and begins giving an example of wheat and tares (weeds). In verse 30 Jesus says, "First gather the tares and bind them in bundles to burn them, but gather the wheat into my barn (storehouse)."

You see, the good ground is the transplanted heart of God in Jesus. The barn (storehouse) is the Kingdom of Heaven. Jesus is talking about seed and the condition of the soil and how this relates to the fruit (the wheat, the harvest).

Now, go back to the tender heart. One can only be in communion with God and receive His presence in the human heart. The only place you can develop a relationship with God and grow is in the heart. Only when you allow God to open the eyes of the heart, will they finally be opened and then you can begin to walk in the Kingdom of God.

The Visions

I saw a bridge going across a deep ravine. I was on the top of a wall looking down at the bridge.

The wall above was 200–300 meters high and 10-15 meters thick. It was made of golden glass. The bridge went to a platform where three gates stood and were guarded by huge white figures with wings. It was then that the Lord showed me a tightrope. On one side was sin and temptation and on the other side was the Lord. He said to me, "I will not allow you to FALL. Do not take the eyes of your heart from me."

This Vision opened to the next Vision — I saw a land frozen in time. I saw trees and flowers and in the distance, a mountain. At the top of the mountain there was a fortress made of the same golden glass. I heard these words, "Then the righteous will shine forth as the sun in the kingdom of their Father. He who has ears to hear, let him hear!" I didn't know it at the time, but this was Matthew 13:43. You see, in this place, the words of Jesus turned to life inside me and opened Visions within me and became life.

The heart has ears, eyes and a mouth. Jesus said in Matthew 13:35, "I will open my mouth in parables, I will utter things, kept secret from the foundation of the world." One can only dream when the foundation of the world was created. Only God (Jesus and the Holy Spirit) knew the secrets He is speaking of as Adam was later created and was in Paradise when he walked with God.

It was Adam who killed the first animal to make clothes to hide his nakedness and in doing so God hid the truth in the Garden of Eden behind thorns. This is why when the truth is revealed to us, it cuts us open. Thus is revelation also — it is a peeling back of our flesh.

> *Likewise, my brethren, you have undergone death as to the Law through the [crucified] body of Christ, so that now you may belong to Another, to Him Who was raised from the dead in order that we may bear fruit for God.*
>
> *When we were living in the flesh (mere physical lives), the sinful passions that were awakened and aroused up by [what] the Law [makes sin] were constantly operating in our natural powers (in our bodily organs, in the sensitive appetites and wills of the flesh), so that we bore fruit for death.*
>
> *But now we are discharged from the Law and have terminated all intercourse with it, having died to what once restrained and held us captive. So now we serve not under [obedience to] the old code of written regulations, but [under obedience to the promptings] of the Spirit in newness [of life].*
>
> *Romans 7:4–6 AMP*

Jesus came here to bring heaven on earth. He was raised from the dead in order that we may bear fruit for God for in Jesus. We have eternal life, our names are written in the Book of Life.

Our spirit has been redressed with the Holy Spirit. This is something that only God can do. Therefore, we have access to Heaven because Jesus is seated there with us at the right hand of the Father. We are with Jesus always — this is what the Word says.

As the world's foundation was created, Adam fell and buried half the truth of the original heart intended for man. God removed the secrets from before the foundation of the world to hide them from Satan. Adam gave Satan entrance into his heart (by shirking man's responsibility for woman and for her actions). This was lost until Jesus came.

In order for us to see the full picture and grasp those secrets held in the heart of the Lord, we must turn to Jesus' words and seek the presence of our Saviour. As there was no death in His heart, nothing could keep Him in the grave. His heart belonged to the Father, as it was the Father's heart. This is the heart we need to have transplanted into our spirits. When we receive this heart, we receive His will (His promises and blessings and kingdom). When we obey this heart, we walk in His will from the inside out. (See Luke 12: 43-44 18:29—30, and 22:46.)

In order to see the Father's heart, we must first see the death of Jesus and realize its reality. We experience the meaning in the words that "no greater love can a man give but to lay down his life for his friend." We must move in reverence to bring and give the knowledge of salvation to God's people for the forgiveness and remission of their sin — God will do the rest.

We are to bring and to give the knowledge of salvation to God's people — that through Him they can find the forgiveness and remission of their sin.

Because of and through the heart of tender mercy and loving—kindness of our God, a Light from on high will dawn upon us and visit [us].

Luke 1:77–78 AMP

In Matthew chapter five, we read one of the most important statements regarding the heart, when Jesus says, "Blessed are the pure of heart, for they shall see God."

Being pure in heart speaks of meekness – but not in the way that many view this word today.

When we look at the word meek, manifested by the Lord and commended to the man of God, the word means THE FRUIT OF POWER. The common assumption is that when man is meek, it is because he cannot help himself. Actually, when a man is meek, he realizes that he has the infinite resources of God at his command. Meekness is the opposite of self–assertiveness and self interest. Meekness is total acquiescence to the Spirit of God because it is not occupied with itself. *Prans* or *Praos*, means gentle or mild. These are feelings of the heart for which there are no words. In heaven, this earthly vocabulary of words is not sufficient. (Just like earthly music is not sufficient for heaven's worship.)

> *When a man is meek, he realizes that he has infinite resources of God at his command*

God reveals himself in His Name, especially in the sanctuary where He causes His name to dwell.

This place (and its secrets) have been kept hidden by the Lord since the fall of man came, plunging the world into darkness. Revelation in the Word of God comes when we recover the memory of those things that were there before the darkness. We receive this revelation through Jesus when we are born again as our names are written in the Lamb's Book of Life! (Jesus is the Lamb.) The whole human race is made up of prodigal sons who are waiting to wake up.

One only has to look at witchcraft (disobedience, rebellion) with its various forms and counterfeit beliefs and practices to see that the whole earth is spellbound with the delusion of a lie. This lie was created by vision that is limited to the fallen state of man and the natural heart. It is bound to the natural limitations of man and his fall when he handed himself to Satan.

Jesus came to change all of that. The heart of Jesus knows no earthly limits and contains the secrets that have been kept hidden from the foundation of the earth. These secrets are only revealed in the new heart God can give us and made known in His word by the Holy Spirit in the of love of God as we remember OUR FIRST LOVE.

Chapter 5

Jokannan and John's Gospel

Unity: One Body, One Heart and One Mind

I want to look at the Gospel of John through the eyes of the heart that God wants to give us. As I begin, I want to quote from the book of Matthew regarding *Jokannan*.

> *For this is he who was spoken of by the prophet Isaiah, saying: "The voice of one crying in the wilderness (desolate and dry places): 'Prepare the way of the LORD; Make His paths straight.'"*

Matthew 3:3 NKJV

The King James Version of the Bible spells this name, *Johanan*. The name *Johanan* means *Yahweh* or *Yahweh has been gracious*. Actually, *Johanan* was the name given to John the Baptist. (This is not the John who wrote the Gospel of John under the inspiration of the Holy Spirit.)

The way *Jokannan* is talking about is the way into the heart. Now in the Gospel of John, the first scripture begins, "In the beginning was the Word, and the Word was with God, and the Word was God. He was in the beginning with God. All things were made through Him, and without Him nothing was made that was made. In Him was life, and the life was the light of men. And the light shines in the darkness, and the darkness did not comprehend it" John 1:1–5 NKJV.

I want to look more closely at these scriptures. Verse two begins with "HE WAS." He was in the beginning with God. Now, the 'Word' of God is masculine. Look at verse one, "In the beginning was the Word, and the Word was with God and the Word WAS God." John 1:14 says, "and the Word became flesh and dwelt among us." This Word was Jesus. Jesus was (is) the Word in John 1:10–11 where it says, "He was in the world, and the world was made through Him, and the world did not know Him. He came to His own, and His own did not receive Him" NKJV. This passage goes on to say, "But as many as received Him, to them He gave the right to become children of God, to those who believe in His name: who were born, not of blood, nor of the will of the flesh, nor of the will of man, but of God" John 1:12–13 NKJV.

This is telling us that if we will accept Him for who He is and receive Him, we will become His children. We are talking about being born of God's will, which is in His heart.

If we continue reading down to verse 18, we find that, "No one has seen God at any time. The only begotten Son, who is in the bosom of the Father, He has declared Him" NKJV. The bosom of the Father is the heart of the Father. This gives a new meaning to John 1:5 where it says, "And the light shines in the darkness, and the darkness did not comprehend it." There is a heart of light and a heart of darkness. The heart of darkness cannot comprehend (understand, grasp or follow) the heart of light.

Now let us return to *Jokannan,* the man. This is the one that the prophet Isaiah declared would be the forerunner of Jesus — that he would prepare the way and point out the Messiah. In John 1 we find the account of *Jokannan* (John the Baptist) as he baptizes Jesus. John had never met Jesus before, but he recognized Him by the Spirit and knew that this was the Son of God.

The next day John saw Jesus coming toward him, and said, "Behold! The Lamb of God who takes away the sin of the world! This is He of whom I said, 'After me comes a Man who is preferred before me, for He was before me.' I did not know Him; but that He should be revealed to Israel, therefore I came baptizing with water" John 1:29–31 NKJV.

"...this is He who baptizes with the Holy Spirit.' And I have seen and testified that this is the Son of God." John 1:33b–34 NKJV

Jesus was the Son of God. Jesus was the heart of God - manifested in flesh, walking, living and breathing. When Jesus was crucified, the very heart of God was sacrificed for us.

John the Baptist was sent before Jesus. He was sent to prepare the way for Jesus to come. In a way, we are a little like John the Baptist. We also have been sent before — in order to prepare others to receive the presence of Christ. In John 3:3 Jesus tells Nicodemus, "you must be born again." In verse five he continues, "Unless one is born of water and the spirit he cannot enter the Kingdom of God."

Zeal is Written on our Hearts

When we receive the Holy Spirit, our body becomes a temple — the temple of the Holy Spirit. (1 Corinthians 6:19.) Jesus' body was also the temple of the Holy Spirit — the place where God dwelt. Jesus had a great deal of reverence for the place where God dwelt. This was evident in the purity of His own flesh as well as in His zeal to maintain the purity of the literal temple that was made of stone and set apart for God's worship. In John 2 we see Jesus driving out moneychangers (merchants) from this temple.

> *"When He had made a whip of cords, He drove them all out of the temple, with the sheep and the oxen, and poured out the changers' money and overturned the tables. And He said to those who sold doves, 'Take these things away! Do not make My Father's house a house of merchandise!' Then His disciples remembered that it was written*, 'Zeal for Your house has eaten Me up.'"*

John 2:15–17 NKJV
**This was written in Psalm 69:9*

Driving out the merchants from the temple was a very bold act. It raised questions in the minds of the Jews. They wondered who He was — that He was so bold to command authority in the very house of God. They asked Him to show them a sign — to prove His authority. Jesus answered them by saying, "Destroy this temple, and in three days I will raise it up." But the Jews mocked Him. They knew it had taken forty–six years to build the temple and to rebuild it from rubble in three days was impossible!

They did not understand that Jesus was talking about His own body — the temple of the Holy Spirit. He was speaking of His death and resurrection — not of stones and mortar.

Later on, after His resurrection, His disciples remembered what had happened in the temple and the answer that Jesus had given them and they believed.

All Things Were Made Through Him (John 1:3)

Jesus was the Word made flesh. We receive power when we receive the tender heart of Jesus. When the heart of the Lord is transplanted in us, the Word of God receives new life and power of it's own as it comes alive in us.

I want to continue the story of Jesus found in John's Gospel. It is beautiful and filled with power and life. It is the story that opens the door for us to receive the heart of God and be made a new creation.

The book of John continues to demonstrate miracles, signs and wonders and the healing power of Jesus. He turns water to wine, feeds five thousand people with only a loaf of bread and a few fish, He heals the sick, walks on water... Many people believe. Others turn away from Him, but all that He does fulfils prophecy and leads to the moment where He is sacrificed for us.

As we come to the Garden of Gethsemane, we find Jesus in prayer. It was a desperate prayer. It was desperation not that the Father would not hear Him, but that He would have time for it to come out of his mouth. This was the prayer spoken just before he went to the Brook Kiddron where he was betrayed and arrested. "Father, I desire that they also whom You gave Me may be with Me where I am, that they may behold My glory which You have given Me; for You loved Me before the foundation of the world" John 17:24 NKJV.

Jesus is talking about a love that was established even before the world was created. He is speaking of a relationship with the Father before the world had even been established. That's why he says, "Oh, righteous father the world has not known you." But He goes on to say, "The love with which you loved me MAY BE IN THEM AND I IN THEM."

Can you receive that!

We have missed the most passionate desire of Jesus – for us to have His heart

Jesus is saying that the Father's heart that is inside of Him should be in us! Just as the Holy Spirit, which is testifying of Jesus and is His presence, should be in us as well.

We have missed the most passionate desire of Jesus – for us to have His heart. Not just His Holy Spirit, but His heart also. To desire His heart to the point where we hate our own dark heart.

I am going to work backwards now, through John to explain. Jesus says;

> "Sanctify them by Your truth. Your Word is truth." John 17:17 NKJV

Jesus was sent as the Word made flesh.

> *"As you sent me into the world, I also have sent them into the world." John 17:18* NKJV

We are God's representatives in the world now. We are the living Word and must be in unity with Jesus. If the Word is to remain pure in us, we must be One with the Father — just as Jesus and the Father are One.

> *Now I am no longer in the world, but these are in the world, and I come to You. Holy Father, keep through Your name those whom You have given Me, that they may be one as We are.*
>
> *John 17:11–12* NKJV

He is talking about us, THE ASSEMBLY, one heart, one heart in Christ, one heart in the Father. In the beginning of this prayer, Jesus is talking about the hearts of men.

> *I pray for them. I do not pray for the world but for those whom You have given Me, for they are Yours. And all Mine are Yours, and Yours are Mine, and I am glorified in them.*
>
> *John 17:9–10* NKJV

The power of this prayer can now be revealed.

> *As You have given Him authority over all flesh, that He should give eternal life to as many as You have given Him. And this is eternal life, that they may know You, the only true God, and Jesus Christ whom You have sent.*
>
> *John 17:2–4* NKJV

This is not just men but their hearts. How else can we be one with the Father unless we have His heart in us? When we look at how we are to overcome this world, it is plainly stated, "In that day you will ask in My name, and I do not say to you that I shall pray the Father for you; for the Father Himself loves you, because you have loved Me, and have believed that I came forth from God" John 16:26–27 NKJV. Looking at this scripture, we realize that we need the transplanted heart of Jesus.

Now, get this! The Father Himself loves us, Why? Because we loved Jesus and believed that He came from God. There is an interchangeable love here. This commandment also was given, that whatever we ask the Father in the Name of Jesus, He will give us provided that we adhere to what Jesus says, "These things I command you, that you love one another."

Follow me back through the Scripture regarding this interchangeable love.

> *You are my friends if you do whatever I command you. John 15:14 NKJV*

> *Greater love has no one than this, than to lay down ones life for his friends. John 15:13 NKJV*

> *This is my commandment, that you love one another as I have loved you. John 15:12 NKJV*

> *As the Father loved Me, I also have loved you; abide in My love. If you keep My commandments, you will abide in My love, just as I have kept My Father's commandments and abide in His love. John 15:9–10 NKJV*

> *If you abide in Me, and My words abide in you, you will ask what you desire, and it shall be done for you. John 15:7 NKJV*

> *Abide in Me, and I in you. As the branch cannot bear fruit of itself, unless it abides in the vine, neither can you, unless you abide in Me. John 15:4 NKJV*

Judas (not Iscariot) said to Him, "Lord, how is it that You will manifest Yourself to us, and not to the world?"
Jesus answered and said to him, "If anyone loves Me, he will keep My word; and My Father will love him, and WE WILL COME TO HIM AND MAKE OUR HOME WITH HIM.
He who does not love Me does not keep My words; and the word which you hear is not Mine but the Father's who sent Me.

John 14:22–24 NKJV

Now, the heart is this home and this home is the keeper of the words. Look carefully at what this progression of scripture offers to us. I must emphasize this because it is Jesus' prayer.

1. Do what I command.

2. My commandment is to love one another as I have loved you.

3. There is no greater love than to lay down your life for a friend. (I gave my life for you!)

4. Abide — dwell in My love. (Just as I dwell in My Father's love.)

5. If you abide in Me (My love) — then My Words abide in you. If My Words abide in you, you can ask whatever you desire and it will be done.

6. Your life can only bear fruit (fulfill purpose and destiny) if you abide in Me.

7. If you love Me and keep My word — then I and My Father will come and make our home with you.

John 14:21 talks of the love of Jesus that we should have. "He who has my commandments and keeps them is he who loves me. And he who loves me will be loved by my Father."

The Power of God's Heart Transplanted in Us

"Most assuredly, I say to you, he who believes in Me, the works that I do he will do also; and greater works than these he will do, because I go to My Father. And whatever you ask in My name, that I will do, that the Father may be glorified in the Son. If you ask anything in My name, I will do it.

John 14:12–14 NKJV

Jesus is saying this very assertively. There is power in His words. If you believe in Him, if you love Him, if you abide in Him, then you will do greater works than He did. Greater works! I can hear you saying, "But Jesus raised the dead, healed the sick, brought joy for sadness, opened blinded eyes...greater works than these?"

Yes! He told you that anything you ask in His name, He will do that the Father may be glorified. The key is the condition of your heart when you ask. When you have His heart, you are in total unity with Him — with the Father. When you are in unity with Him, the things you ask for are completely in the will of God. It is only when you have a divided heart and are not abiding in His love that you pray prayers that go unanswered.

Power comes from the Oneness of heart. Jesus was One with the Father. So, everything that Jesus said and did was in God's authority. The One who did the mighty works was GOD — dwelling IN Jesus.

Do you not believe that I am in the Father, and the Father in Me? The words that I speak to you I do not speak on My own authority; but the Father who dwells in Me does the works.

John 14:10 NKJV

The only way we have access to the Father (to the Father's heart) is THROUGH Jesus.

> *"I am the way, the truth, and the life. No one comes to the Father except through Me.* John 14:6 NKJV

Jesus has prepared a place for us to be received in the Father's heart.

Jesus has prepared a place for us to be received in the Father's heart

Let not your heart be troubled; you believe in God, believe also in Me. In My Father's house are many mansions; if it were not so, I would have told you. I go to prepare a place for you. And if I go and prepare a place for you, I will come again and receive you to Myself; that where I am, there you may be also.

John 14:1—4 NKJV

Jesus is in the bosom of the Father, seated at the right hand of the Father, in the place of power. He just promised you that where He is, you would be also. This is exciting!

The Blessing of the Transplanted Heart of Jesus

Through Jesus, the Father has given all things to us. All authority and all power. This brings me back to what Paul said, "Blessed be the God and Father of our Lord Jesus Christ, who has blessed us with every spiritual blessing in the heavenly places in Christ."

Ephesians 1:3 NKJV.

We have been given EVERY spiritual blessing in the heavenly places in Christ. This is beyond our comprehension. And yet, if we grasp just a small glimpse of what this means, our lives will be transformed forever. If we allow Christ's heart to live in us, we will dwell with Him, His words will be in our mouth and we will do greater works. We will walk with God and know God. We will be conformed to His image and have the mind of Christ. We will walk in abundant blessing and know the joy of living each day in the destiny of God!

The Fallen State of the Heart

This is revealed by the words of Isaiah the Prophet, "Who has believed our report? And to whom has the arm of the LORD been revealed? Isaiah 53:1 NKJV

This is fulfilled in the book of John 12:40, "He has blinded their eyes and hardened their hearts, Lest they should see with their eyes, Lest they should understand with their hearts and turn, So that I should heal them."

The Healing of the Heart

He who loves his life (heart) will lose it,
and he who hates his life in this world will
keep it for eternal life. John 12:25 NKJV

You will receive eternal life if you hate your life to the point of loving Jesus' life. We come to a place of knowing His righteousness that is in His heart and His ways are manifested in us so much that the darkness of our own natural heart becomes hateful to us. We are aware of this because we experience how difficult it is to focus on Jesus for more than just a few hours with our fallen hearts. Even Judas, who sold everything he had to follow the Lord and who was chosen of the Lord, was rebuked by Jesus before he betrayed him for dividing his attention. (John 12:8)

When we have the Lord's heart, we have Him always. Even if we don't realize it in our minds, the heart rules the flesh because it is constantly being fed by God.

Our physical heart, the one coursing blood through our veins, is our life. But our spiritual heart is dead until we receive the heart of Jesus. In John 11:25–26 Jesus says, "I am the resurrection and the life. He who believes in Me, though he may die, he shall live. And whoever lives and believes in Me shall never die."

When Jesus raised Lazarus from the dead, He thanked the Father because He had heard Him, and because He always heard Him. God always heard Jesus because Jesus had the Father's heart. God had put his heart into Jesus so that the Word was made flesh. The Word was made flesh so that we could receive it because we are made of flesh (even though we have a spirit).

The father gave us His heart and when we give our heart to the Father we can see the power of being one with the Father.

> *My Father, who has given them to Me, is greater than all; and no one is able to snatch them out of My Father's hand. I and My Father are one."* John 10:29–30 NKJV

This gives a whole new meaning to those who feel they can lose their salvation. It also changes the perspective of those who believe the devil can attack them while they are in the Father's hand. HE is greater — no one (not even Satan) can snatch them out of the Father's hand! It is a revelation of the heart.

Jesus is the Shepherd and the Door is the Heart

> *Most assuredly, I say to you, he who does not enter the sheepfold by the door, but climbs up some other way, the same is a thief and a robber. But He who enters by the door is the shepherd of the sheep. To him the doorkeeper opens and the sheep hear His voice and he calls His own sheep by Name and when He brings out His own sheep He goes before them and the sheep follow Him for they know His voice."*
>
> John 10:1–3 NKJV

The doorkeeper is God, who gives those to Jesus. When He is talking about the sheep by name, He is talking about the names written in the Lamb's Book of Life. When He talks about the sheep following Him because they know his voice, He is talking about receiving the voice of God in the heart. They receive His voice in the heart by being faithful and receiving that Word and commandment by the Holy Spirit and placed in the heart of God.

The heart we have spoken about as the door is the heart of Jesus. (John 10:7 – "I am the door of the sheep.") Therefore, in order for us to belong to Him we must have His heart. He goes on to say, "I am the door. If anyone enters by Me he will be saved and will go in and out and find pasture." **WE MUST SETTLE THIS ONCE AND FOR ALL IN OUR HEARTS.** Jesus is our head and our heart pastor. When He says we will "find pasture," it means that we will be fed as Jesus' heart is constantly fed by God.

> *I am the good shepherd. The good shepherd gives His life for the sheep. John 10:11 NKJV*
>
> *And other sheep I have which are not of this fold; them also I must bring, and they will hear My voice; and there will be ONE flock and ONE shepherd. John 10:16 NKJV*
>
> *The LORD is my shepherd; I shall not want. (I shall not want because everything has been give to me.) Psalm 23:1 NKJV*

The area of *"pasturing"* is a place that is now being reformed by the Lord's chosen apostles. It is being returned to the original purpose it was destined for. We are all constantly being renewed and formed into a new image of His likeness.

The Ears of the Heart

> *He who is of God hears God's words; therefore you do not hear, because you are not of God." John 8:47 NKJV*

Jesus was talking to the Pharisees just after He told them that they were of their father, the devil, who was a murderer from the beginning and does not stand in truth. So, the reason they could not hear God's words was because they were not of God. When a person belongs to God, he is able to hear God speak.

The Pharisees could not hear God and they did not love Jesus. This was because the devil was their father and not God.

> *"If God were your Father, you would love Me, for I proceeded forth and came from God; John 8:42 NKJV*

Now, these Pharisees were Jews, Abraham's descendants and therefore, they were SUPPOSED to be children of God.

> *"I know that you are Abraham's descendants, but you seek to kill Me, because My word has no place in you. John 8:37 NKJV*

These men had no heart to receive His word. They were not sons of God. In John 8:35 we learn that although slaves come and go, a son abides forever in the House of God. We were slaves to sin, but sons to God! "And you shall know the truth and the truth shall make you free" John 8:32. The truth (Jesus) set us free (as slaves) from sin.

The Power of Unity

> *And He who sent Me is with Me. The Father has not left Me alone, for I always do those things that please Him." John 8:29 NKJV*

The Father needs no help from us. Our purpose and His desire is only that we please him — we make Him happy. This gives new meaning to "where there are two or more gathered, there shall I be also." When the Father is in our hearts and we are gathered together, He will be there. Look at this in terms of the collective body of Christ, having the transplanted heart of Jesus in each person, the power is limitless! God is one head and there are millions in unity with Jesus on earth.

~~~~~~~~~

"Most assuredly, I say to you, he
who believes in Me,
the works that I do
he will do also; and
greater works than these he will do,
because I go to My Father.
And whatever you ask in
My name, that I will do,
that the Father may be
glorified in the Son.
If you ask anything in
My name, I will do it.
John 14:12-14

~~~~~~~~~

Chapter 6

~~~~~~~~~

The Door and the New Heart

I know your works, that you are neither cold nor hot. I could wish you were cold or hot.

So then, because you are lukewarm, and neither cold nor hot, I will vomit you out of My mouth.

Because you say, 'I am rich, have become wealthy, and have need of nothing' — and do not know that you are wretched, miserable, poor, blind, and naked —   I counsel you to buy from Me gold refined in the fire, that you may be rich; and white garments, that you may be clothed, that the shame of your nakedness may not be revealed; and anoint your eyes with eye salve, that you may see.

As many as I love, I rebuke and chasten. Therefore be zealous and repent.

*Behold, I stand at the door and knock. If anyone
hears My voice and opens the door, I will come
in to him and dine with him, and he with Me.*

*To him who overcomes I will grant to sit with
Me on My throne, as I also overcame and
sat down with My Father on His throne."*

Revelation 3:15–21 NKJV

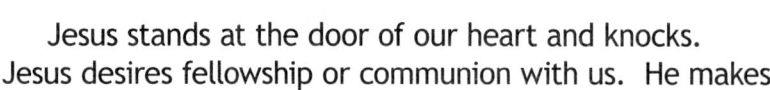

Jesus stands at the door of our heart and knocks.
Jesus desires fellowship or communion with us. He makes
the invitation, we have but to accept it and join Him.

Many people today feel that they do not need God.
They have plenty of worldy goods, a stable career, a
respectable family and friends, or they have too little
and are happy to blame others for their condition and
look to the government or some other entity to take
care of them. In the passage above, we learn that
God knows how wretched, miserable, poor, blind and
naked we truly are. He counsels us to buy gold from
HIM — gold that has been refined in the fire that we
may be rich. He tells us to buy white garments (pure,
spotless garments) that we may be clothed and not
have the shame of our nakedness revealed. He tells
us to anoint our eyes with salve so that we may see.
These are all spiritual conditions — not physical ones.

The Lord goes on to tell us that he rebukes and
chastens (corrects) those He loves. Just as we
correct our children, motivated by love for them
and looking after their best interests, protection
and opportunities. God tells us to be zealous and
repent. How many truly zealous (ardent, dedicated,

devoted, passionate) people have you encountered? Repentance simply means to turn around — to cease from your present course and turn toward God.

BE ZEALOUS

Be zealous. This literally means to be marked by active interest and enthusiasm. A zealous people are earnest in their desire and pursuit of God. And even though there are churches who are on fire for God, if we can consider the assembly of all churches as a single grouping, sadly we see a lukewarm body — not a zealous one. It is easy to see why the Lord is starting to shake the church from the ground up. In Revelation 3:15 He says, "So then, because you are lukewarm, neither cold nor hot, I will vomit you out of my mouth." There will be a sifting which will take place of such magnitude that we have never seen before. During this sifting, those who have not repented and given the Lord their whole hearts will find that they have no place in the Kingdom of Heaven. What does this mean?

It means that the promises of God found in His Word can only be honoured when we come to Him with our whole hearts. There has been a condition in the church that has been tolerated. There has been evidence of a spirit of immobility and controlling spirits that have been allowed too much freedom among God's people. These shall now be commanded to leave. Those who come to the Lord and present their heart as a sacrifice to Him, turning their back on efforts to please men and the establishments built by men (called the church) — only these shall be worthy of His presence.

St. Augustine, in his book, The City of God, says that "sin is vice." A vice is something that holds us. It grips

with increasing strength. So, it sits in the heart —
buried in the flesh. It can compel us by its power, as the
gripping pressure is steadily increased. That relentless
pressure gives a demonic entity opportunity to move
into that area and take control. Then, the demon having
entrance to this area, can supercharge that area with
sin, temporally blinding us from all responsibility and
the past reality shown to us by our heart's original
intention. This becomes a stronghold, a new worldy
reality contained in and held captive by the vice of this particular area of sin.

When we walk in sin, we give legal rights to the entrance of sickness and disease into our mind and even within our physical body

Sin is separation from God. The Bible says that the wages of sin is death...spiritual death. Sin brings death to the spirit. When we walk in sin, we give legal rights to the entrance of sickness and disease into our mind and even within our physical body. But the man of God is dead to sin because his heart is conformed to the Lord. He has been changed from the inside out by the Holy Spirit and is therefore protected by God and Jesus Himself.

BUILD THE NEW INNER MAN FROM THE HEART OUTWARDS

The importance of building the new inner man from the heart outwards has always been neglected. This change starts by asking Jesus to give us His heart, for there is the spring of eternal life. There begins in us the power of creation and all the promises of the Father and the Kingdom of heaven. There begins eternal life and what I can only describe as the total presence of the Word.

THE NEW MAN IS VICTORIOUS

We should pray that we receive Jesus' heart and that the inner man be rebuilt from it. Having accepted Jesus' heart as our new heart, we will now we want to have His arms, His legs, His eyes, His ears and His mouth. We want Him to be in us in all of our being. We put on the incorruptible mind of Christ (1 Corinthians 2:16) and we suit up in His armour (Galatians 6:11) being dressed by God and equipped with all the promises of the Father. This establishes us in the third heaven — grounded in the third heaven, the place of victory and invincibility. It is the place of being established at His right hand.

The problem we face is this. We have seen a birth of the inner man because people receive salvation, but this is with their old hearts. They try to change the old heart under the guidance of an old church system standing on what has gone before in the past, unable to move into a better future. Because the inner man has only the old eyes, ears and mouth and old heart it is barely able to stand. They are unprepared soldiers, warriors without weapons. They put on their armour with prayers of desperation and stand on a battle field in the second heaven. This is the battlefield of angels and demons. This is a battlefield filled with horrors and a place where, when we venture unequipped and ill prepared, the enemy can lock us into and feed us fear which can lead to deceptions powerful enough to destroy us.

God is a God of war, but we must remember that the battle is the Lord's, not ours alone! (1 Samuel 17:47.) We must understand and believe that the battle is already won. Battles rage on, but the war was won when the Lord said, "it is accomplished," as He died on the cross. Our victory is already secure.

[God] disarmed the principalities and powers that were ranged against us and made a bold display and public example of them, in triumphing over them in Him and in it [the cross]. Colossians 2:15 AMP

Too many Christians are simply playing war. This can be disastrous. When men play around, armed with anything other than God's armour, with ANY other purpose than obedience to God's will, they open themselves to attack that they are no match for. Bravado, misunderstanding and false doctrine have led men to boldly (yet carelessly) rebuke powers and principalities, even confronting Satan himself. Armed with the wrong weapons, without fully embracing God's power or protection, it has cost them their very lives. An attack from Satan without the covering of God is a serious thing. It is unwise to go about, casually boasting about authority and taking on the enemy. Luke 10:20 admonishes not to rejoice that demons and spirits are subject to us — but rather to rejoice that our names have been recorded in heaven!

> *Put on the whole armour of God, that ye may be able to stand against the wiles of the devil.*
>
> *For we wrestle not against flesh and blood, but against principalities, against powers, against the rulers of the darkness of this world, against spiritual wickedness in high places.*
>
> *Wherefore take unto you the whole armour of God, that ye may be able to withstand in the evil day, and having done all, to stand.*
>
> *Ephesians 6:11–13 KJV*

When we put on God's armour we are protected. The armour of God means that our loins are girded with truth. We have the breastplate of righteousness. Our feet are shod with the preparation of the Gospel of peace. We have taken up the shield of faith and we have put on the helmet of salvation and picked up the sword of the spirit which is the Word of God.

Ephesians 6 says that, "we wrestle not against flesh and blood, but against principalities, powers and the rulers of darkness and against spiritual wickedness in high places." Colossians 2 says that Jesus "disarmed the principalities and powers and made a bold and public display of them when He triumphed over the cross." Which is it? Do we war or is the war won? The war is won.

IT IS FINISHED

Is the battle over? The ultimate battle is, but the daily battles still must be fought. Still, we have no fear of the enemy because he is a defeated foe and we have the authority of Christ to walk in victory over him. Does this mean we can forget about our armour? No. The threat remains. Satan continues to try to defeat us, even though he has lost. Why do we need protection if there is no threat?

The work of the cross was (and is) an eternal reality. God knew you before you were in your mother's womb and was able to call you by name. Only God can understand the scope of eternity — we can barely grasp its reality. The Bible states that Jesus was slain before the foundation of the world — but the physical experience of the cross was a recordable moment in the history of time. But time does not limit that moment. Its reality stretches across the entire scope of eternity.

When Christ's death and resurrection were completed — our redemption was purchased. Our ability to live a victorious life, free from the ravages of sin was secured in eternity. And yet, it is up to us to walk out this privilege day by day.

In Colossians 2, we learn that Jesus defeated Satan, disarmed principalities and powers and made a bold and public display of them when He triumphed over the cross. Where was this display — in Jerusalem's downtown square? No, it was in the heavenlies, it was in eternity. Now we walk out this victory day by day.

So, the threat of attack from principalities and powers remains as long as we dwell on the earth. They will be active until the moment of the last judgement when they are sealed in hell with no more licence to roam. However, the threat of defeat from these enemies is ONLY a threat if we allow ourselves (heart, mind or spirit) to be outside of God's protection or not submitted to His will. When our heart is surrendered and our will is yielded to God we are in union with Him — and it is not possible for God to be defeated by the enemy.

Those who have fallen to the enemy have done so as a result of a lack of understanding or because of false teaching. The church of today (as an establishment) has too often bullied young men of God into being mentored and fathered by men who are without the spirit of God. The Word of God says, "My people perish for lack of knowledge" Hosea 4:6. So much of the church has become a religious entity, a "form of godliness" rather than an expression of God. Often, the young Christian has been dragged into this, the victim of a deceiver which has robbed him from the first commandment, "You shall love the LORD your God with all your heart, with all your soul, and with all your strength" Deuteronomy 6:5 NKJV.

When this foundation has been corrupted, we only have God's grace. This again unveils the meaning of the word *Jokannan — Yawheh has been gracious*. John's message was, "Make straight the way of the Lord." We can only do this if we speak truth. Corrupting the message with religious forms will not release God's grace. And by that grace we are given license to speak.

THE MOUTHPIECE OF GOD

Paul says that of all the gifts of the Holy Spirit, we are to want prophecy more than any other. In

Corinthians, Paul is teaching ALL the churches (not just the church in Corinth) about the diversities of the gifts and ministries of the Holy Spirit by the Lord. In Corinthians 13:2 he says, "And though I have the gift of prophecy and understand all mysteries and all knowledge, and though I have all faith so that I could remove mountains but have not love, I am nothing."

In Ephesians 2, Paul speaks about God making us alive and that He has "raised us up together, and made us sit together in the heavenly places in Christ Jesus, THAT IN THE AGES TO COME HE MIGHT SHOW THE EXCEEDING RICHES OF HIS GRACE IN HIS KINDNESS TOWARD US IN CHRIST JESUS" Ephesians 2:6–7 NKJV.

For through Him we both have access by one Spirit to the Father.

Now, therefore, you are no longer strangers and foreigners, but fellow citizens with the saints and members of the household of God, having been built on the foundation of the apostles and prophets, Jesus Christ Himself being the chief cornerstone, in whom the whole building, being fitted together, grows into a holy temple in the Lord, in whom you also are being built together for a dwelling place of God in the Spirit. Ephesians 2:18–22 NKJV

A NEW BREED

So we are to prophesy our blessings as the Holy Spirit leads us in our call. We are to live out the prophecy — so our blessings are manifested along the way. Take heed, the Lord is calling up a new generation and a new breed of believer. This new breed will not be struggling to make it through the day, burdened down with the cares of the world, taunted by the enemy and trying his best just to make it through. This new breed will be victorious! This believer will have the heart of God beating in him. He will understand his place at the right hand of the Father and will delight to do the will of God unhindered by doubt and disbelief or distracted by attack.

The name Jeremiah comes from the name **Yirmeyahu** or **Yirmeyah**. It literally means, *Yahweh throws*. The footnotes of the New King James Version says, "perhaps in the sense of laying a foundation, Yahweh (one of God's Names), establishes, appoints and sends." The first chapter of Jeremiah is discussing the call of the Prophet.

In the past, prophets prophesied largely to the church for the church, primarily to comfort the church. The new prophet of God shall be prophesying as the voice of God and his word shall be from God and it shall be a calling to the hearts of men. It shall be as one crying in the wilderness, make straight paths for the Lord. John's message was, "Make straight the way of the Lord." This is the call to the Kingdom of God. God wants us to be His mouthpiece like Jesus was.

The new prophet of God shall be prophesying as the voice of God and his word shall be from God

Then the LORD put forth His hand and touched my mouth, and the LORD said to me:

"Behold, I have put My words in your mouth.

See, I have this day set you over the nations and over the kingdoms,

To root out and to pull down,

To destroy and to throw down,

TO BUILD AND TO PLANT." Jeremiah 1:9—10

In the fourth century, there was a rising up of key men by the Holy Spirit. Great men such as St. Frances of Asissi and St. Augustine of Hippo (to name two). In later centuries more would come, Luther, Calvin, Knox and Tyndale. In the 19th and 20th centuries we have seen men like Smith Wigglesworth, Kenneth Hagin, and others of great faith come forth as well. But these, and others like them were just the first fruits of what is yet to come. Their message came to prepare the way for others who would come later... who would come in this day. And this new generation will open up the power of God on earth like never before.

THE KEY

The key to opening the power of God on earth will be for the church to repent. As it does, it will acknowledge that all that has come before has been first fruits. Much of what these first fruit ministries have achieved has been stolen from God and His church. They must be given back to the Lord in repentance. The church must ask for these first fruits ministries of faith and of grace to be restored in great measure to purchase the gold and the white garments spoken of in Revelation 3:17—18. The church must do this so that it can return to its first love and recognize the Lord Jesus as the head of the church — over all things through a new heart, the transplanted heart of Jesus in us. Our body shall therefore be dead to sin.

> *But you are those who have continued with Me in My trials. And I bestow upon you a kingdom, just as My Father bestowed one upon Me, that you may eat and drink at My table in My kingdom, and sit on thrones judging the twelve tribes of Israel." Luke 22:28—30 NKJV*

> *And the Lord said, "Simon, Simon (Peter, Peter)! Indeed, Satan has asked for you, that he may sift you as wheat. But I have prayed for you, that your faith should not fail; and when you have RETURNED TO ME, strengthen your brethren." Luke 22:31—32 NKJV*

Jesus said, "return to me." We must return to our first love. Each morning when we wake up, we must address that heart of Jesus within us, carried there by the Holy Spirit. We must ask that heart, "What is it that you will reveal to me today?" Each day we must again embrace our blessed Father and thank Him with a whole heart.

~~~~~~~~~~

*Thou hast created
us for Thyself,
and our heart is not quiet
until it rests in Thee.*

Saint Augustine

~~~~~~~~~~

Chapter 7

The Total Presence of the Word

There is power in the Word of God. When we experience the total presence of God's Word, the authority of God's promise to us is overwhelming. There is energy and life in the Word of God. There is power in the totality of the Word of God.

With all this power and authority available to every Believer, what keeps us from experiencing victory in every situation? What could possibly keep us from experiencing the fullness of God's promise and purpose?

Just as every good thought, act and deed originates in the divine will of God, sin originates in our will. Therefore, once we see that all sin was forgiven on the cross — past, present and future, we realize that we have been set free from sin — from the curse of the law. In Galatians chapter three, the Apostle Paul explains that Christ has fulfilled the law — replacing it as our "tutor" by the work of faith. This means that we have the power to overcome sin! It isn't about breaking "rules," it is about taking on the character of Christ in our hearts. If we are merely living by a set of rules, our life is nothing but dead works. The issue is our heart. Our heart must be one with God, and that oneness gives life to the Word. We are then fed by the spirit, which is the Holy Spirit.

> *...fools die for lack of wisdom.*
> *Proverbs 10:21 NKJV*

> *My people are destroyed for lack*
> *of knowledge... Hosea 4:6 KJV*

Few things are as destructive as bad teaching. A lack of wisdom can reduce the power of the Word of God in a person's life to nothing. Many people, armed with only a small piece of Scripture, rush headlong into battle — rebuking principalities and powers, only to return defeated and discouraged. It is vital to walk in the totality of Scripture. It is dangerous to grab a small piece without understanding the full purpose of God and rush into doctrine or practice — quoting Scripture, but lacking wisdom, understanding and authority.

Scripture tells us (in Matthew 28:18) that ALL AUTHORITY has been given to Jesus. It also tells us (in John 14:12) that those who believe in Jesus will do GREATER WORKS than Jesus. Many people grab this with excitement and jump into situations they are not prepared for — brashly claiming the authority of God and commanding things in the heavenlies that come from THEIR OWN MIND or PURPOSE — not from the will of God. The context of the authority given to Jesus in Matthew 28:18 was to "Go and make disciples of all nations, baptizing them in the name of the Father, the Son and the Holy Spirit." This is the condition of the authority. This is the purpose — dominion; to make disciples of all nations. He continues, telling them to teach others to observe the things He has commanded them to do.

Men and women who foolishly claim God's authority without God's purpose are so easily stripped of their faith. Everything (from car collisions to sudden illnesses to financial or family pressures) attacks their focus and determination and causes them to fear and to doubt. Some even deny God altogether and totally abandon their faith. They wallow in confusion and pity, giving root to bitterness and damaging the kingdom with the sourness of their wounded pride. Only when we walk in obedience to the will of the Father and our heart is in union with Jesus do we possess the authority given to Jesus by the Father. We walk in this union, THEN we exercise this authority in order to accomplish God's purpose in the earth. In this union, submitted to the will of the Father, there is no limit to the power of God within us.

Jesus' final comment in this discourse is, "And surely I am with you always, even to the end of the age." This encourages us. When we receive His heart, we receive His will with gladness. We are then in a place to allow the Holy Spirit to move in us as Jesus moved in the earth. That is, Jesus always had the Father's heart in Him. It was His prayer that the Father's heart be in us also.

Our mission on earth is not to go about carelessly rebuking powers and principalities — not even to go about rebuking the devil himself. WHEN WE ACT, WALK, BELIEVE AND OBEY ACCORDING TO OUR OFFICE AND OUR CALL, WE SHALL HAVE ALL AUTHORITY. (As described in Matthew 28:18–20.)

There are spiritual battles raging. (These occur in the Second Heaven). This is a place where angels contend with the enemy. Venturing into this battlefield without a direct Word from God can cause irreparable damage to our spirits. The most devoted Christian with the purest heart cannot long sustain combat with principalities and powers. We were not created specifically for this arena. Sooner or later, in a moment of unguarded flesh, fatigue or distraction, the enemy will wield his blow. This is why it is SO important to remain in obedience to the will of the Father. When we do the Father's will, we walk in His power and His authority.

When we do the Father's will, we walk in His power and authority

We are in the world, but not of the world. The world hates us because it hated Him. (John 15:18-26) When we walk with God, we walk in a place of victory, the place of His right hand (the Third Heaven). From this place of authority, we are to subdue the earth, putting every activity and possession of the enemy underfoot — just as Jesus put the enemy under His feet.

When we are in the place of the throne of God, we can venture into the Third Heaven, the place where all battles have been won.

How do we walk in there?

THIS IS ONLY POSSIBLE WITH THE KING.

How will He let us in there?

HE KNOWS US BY OUR HEARTS.

How do we have this confidence with Him?

BECAUSE HE KNOWS AND TRUSTS US AND BECAUSE WE HAVE RECEIVED HIS HEART.

Those who go to God everyday in love and meekness in front of the enemy, shall be vanquished. You see, if you decide to fight the Lord's battles, you will not give Him a chance to do battle for you. Sadly, this is exactly what the body of Christ has been doing while the enemy has been saying "come on, have a go." This is one reason why we have not realized all the promises of the word in this context of victory.

Not only is the Lord's head detached from its body, but the body is scattered and has failed the head. The body (the church) is going off in all directions and fighting battles between his own members. The arms are fighting the feet and the ears are fighting the mouth. Spirits of pride and self importance have entered the body and have caused a state of chaos. How many times have we seen missions and crusades into countries, where one ministry will not help another? Jealousy, doctrinal differences or a spirit of independence keep the body from functioning as a united force and the harvest is lost while the labourers flex their muscles and boast of their exploits.

Many ministries are focused on building their kingdom rather than God's kingdom. They build a house of merchandise rather than a house of worship. The cycle goes on and on. Wherever we have seen men and women of God walk in their true office, we have seen thousands and even hundreds of thousands come to the Lord.

When the body is submitted to the head, we have seen God manifest His presence in the earth. We have seen Him "roll up his sleeves" and "go to work." When this happens, what we see is not merely revival, it is an AWAKENING.

Look at the final scripture verse in the book of Matthew. Jesus says, "Lo, I am with you always, even unto the end of the age." There you have it. He is here now. We do not need to wait for Him to come, He is here now. In the scope of eternity, the outcome of every single battle is known — and we win! God has given us the victory — even over the battles we have yet to see.

All things in the book of Revelation have been accomplished in eternity. Death will be swallowed up in victory as we walk into Eternity. For now, we have mortal bodies and God has given us the choice to choose Him as our first Love, or to choose service to Satan. The choice is mandatory — we MUST choose. We will choose. When we venture away from the love of God, that is a choice. When we walk into darkness into a place where the enemy is hiding in shadow, that is a choice.

True, we are supposed to carry a sword (which is the word of God) and a shield, which is faith, our confidence that God is what He promised to be. In Boyd's Dictionary, the word shield is defined as cover. In Psalm 91 the Lords says He will cover us with His wings. The word of God also says that He is our shield and buckler. In Psalm 23 the word of God says that we are to fear no evil. We are not to be afraid of the enemy.

THE MOST IMPORTANT PRAYER JESUS PRAYED

Jesus prayed for us. He told the twelve apostles that He prayed for them and for those who would come to Him. You must understand that you are personally covered by Jesus. He is your fortress and strong tower. He is your shield and your deliverer!

Being covered by a church or by an apostolic covering is important. But anyone who thinks that this covering is sufficient is wrong. We MUST be covered by God. We MUST be covered by the Word of God. The prayers of man alone are insufficient to stop the devil. We need the prayer covering of the Holy Spirit.

In the same way, the Spirit helps us in our weakness. We do not know what we ought to pray for, but the Spirit himself intercedes for us with groans that words cannot

> *express. And He who searches our hearts*
> *knows the mind of the Spirit, because the*
> *Spirit intercedes for the saints in accordance*
> *with God's will. Romans 8:26 - 27* NIV

A WARNING

I strongly advise against reading much literature pertaining to descriptions and visions of the battle field in the Second Heaven and it's horrors — Christian or otherwise. This is not something our attention should be absorbed with. If you look for darkness, you will surely find it. If you focus on the Light — the darkness will flee. Demon-hunting, even in the Name of Jesus smacks of the Occult. It occurs in hidden places, shrouded in darkness. It is the place where spirits create nightmares and fears. It is the place where dark powers live and it is a place where they have power — even if limited. I am not saying that you will never encounter an attack or deal with a demonic force or influence. What I am saying is that you don't need to go looking for a fight. Walk with God. Walk in obedience to the Father. Realize that your vision is limited — you cannot comprehend or even see eternity no matter how hard you try. Our place of safety AND effectiveness is when we are seated at the right hand of God, in the place of Victory under the covering of the Father.

We are to declare victory. We are to walk in victory. We are to live in victory. The place of victory is with God, seated with Him, walking in faith and obedience. This is the place of power. This is the place of promise. This is the place where the power of the Word of God comes alive in us, the place where the fullness of God is at work in our lives. In this place, the promises of God are fulfilled and we live in the favour of God.

THE THREE NETS OF SATAN

Among the writings discovered in the Dead Sea Scrolls, is a passage that speaks of the three nets of Satan.

They are defined as:

Profanity of the Temple

Fornication

Love of Riches

The conclusion offered states that whoever did not fall into first net, fell into the second. And, if he somehow escaped the second net, then he fell into third. This describes a somewhat hopeless situation. Satan has set his snare for God's people and is ready to trip or to trap them by any means necessary. Thus, being armoured up, being strong in the Word, and having the heart of Jesus within your heart provides you the kind of safety you need and the victory He has won.

BEING CHANGED

The Word of God could only "be" (or accomplish) its full potential in the heart of Jesus. The Word of God says, "He was the Word made flesh." It is the power of God's Word that changes the heart of man.

When sickness in the physical body occurs, the common response is to turn to doctors, or alternative medicine or to some other limited healing exercises like yoga or transcendental meditation. Some may even turn to a "religion" for comfort or to find a solution. Given enough pain, people will seek out therapy, pain management or other kinds of help such as acupuncture, hypnosis or *Reiki*. All of these things enter the body from the outside in, but the Word of God changes us from the inside out. The Word of God was written by the Holy Spirit. We have been given the promise to receive it and we can receive it once we are saved. But to see the full fruit of the Word of God, we must ask Jesus for His Heart. Not only did everything that was created proceed from that heart, but the Word of God itself came from that heart. When we receive that new heart, we return to God.

The Word will teach us more than our normal hearts could ever comprehend

Does this mean we lose our identity? No. It means that we are going to act on the Word in a different way — with new understanding. It means that the Word will teach us more than our normal hearts could ever comprehend. Having the heart of God puts the flesh into a place where it can not interfere in the execution of God's Word or hinder the movement of the Holy Spirit. It is a foundation of faith, which we were meant to have thousands of years ago. It is something which I believe the original apostles of Jesus and even some of the early church fathers were privy to in the first through the fourth centuries.

CAPTURE GOD'S FULL ATTENTION

So let's approach God and see if we can catch the Father's attention.

*Therefore, my brethren, you also were made
to die to the Law through the body of Christ,
that you might be joined to another, to Him
who was raised from the dead, that we might
bear fruit for God. For while we were in the
flesh, the sinful passions, which were aroused
by the Law, were at work in the members
of our body to bear fruit for death. But now
we have been released from the Law, having
died to that by which we were bound, so that
we serve in newness of the Spirit and not in
oldness of the letter. Romans 7:4–6 NASB*

We belong to Him, the One who was raised from the
dead in order that we may bear fruit for God. In Jesus we
have eternal life. Our names have been written in the
Lamb's Book of Life and our spirit has been redressed.

GO, MAKE DISCIPLES

*"And you, child, will be called the
prophet of the Highest;*

*For you will go before the face of
the Lord to prepare His ways,*

To give knowledge of salvation to His people

By the remission of their sins,

Through the tender mercy of our God,

*With which the Dayspring from
on high has visited us;*

*To give light to those who sit in
darkness and the shadow of death,*

*To guide our feet into the way of
peace." Luke 1:76 – 79 NKJV*

This Scripture was spoken to Zechariah concerning his son, John the Baptist. This is exactly what we are to do. Didn't Jesus tell us in Matthew that we are to "go and make disciples of all the Nations"? We are to give knowledge of Salvation to His people by the forgiveness and remission of their sins, through the tender mercy and loving kindness of our God.

A light from on high will dawn upon us and visit us. "Blessed are the pure in heart, for they shall see God" Matthew 5:8 NKJV. God is light! We are to give this light to those who sit in darkness and the shadow of death. This light will guide our feet into the way of peace.

> *"Have faith in God. For assuredly, I say to you, whoever says to this mountain, 'Be removed and be cast into the sea,' and does not doubt in his heart, but believes that those things he says will be done, he will have whatever he says. Therefore I say to you, whatever things you ask when you pray, believe that you receive them, and you will have them. Mark 11:22b–24 NKJV*

Let this mountain be your old heart and its burdens. Have faith in God and believe. Ask God to replace your old heart with His heart and it WILL be done!

When we walk in the path Jesus prepares for us in the spiritual realm, we walk in the same path that John the Baptist walked. We fulfill the prophecy in making straight the way of the Lord as we give knowledge of Salvation of His people by the remission of their sins and as we give light to those who sit in darkness and the shadow of death. When we are doing this, we shall have the full attention of God. We shall have His full attention to fulfill all His promises, to receive all His healing, to receive all His prosperity and blessing, and we will see a happy Father.

OUR DEFENSE

The prophet Jeremiah spoke of a remnant that would be from the house of God in the latter days. We are the remnant God was speaking about in chapter 23. He has promised us the safety of the fold, the place of refuge, He has promised that we will be fruitful and increase. He says we will fear no more, nor be lacking.

In Luke 12 we are told again not to be afraid of those who could kill the body, after all, once they have extinguished life in the body, what more can they do? Rather, we are to fear the One who has the power to send that soul to hell after death. God has the very hairs on our head numbered and cares about our every move.

He has equipped us with a ready defense. He has promised that we never need to worry about what to say to man. He has promised that in that very moment, the Holy Spirit will teach us what we ought to say.

And so we see that God desires for us to live in the total presence and power of His Word. His plan is one of a victorious life, filled with the promise and blessing of God. It is His pleasure that we, His children, should choose to love Him. It is His pleasure as our Father, to bestow His perfect love, protection and blessing on us.

~~~~~~~~~~~~~~~~

*Won't you
surrender your old heart
and receive
His heart today?*

~~~~~~~~~~~~~~~~

Chapter 8

~~~~~~~~~~

The First Commandment

Jesus said to him, "'You shall love the LORD your God with all your heart, with all your soul, and with all your mind.' This is the first and great commandment. Matthew 22:37—38 NKJV

God is calling us to return to our first love. We must return to the first (and greatest) commandment — to love God with all our heart, soul and mind. In the book of Jeremiah, there is a theme of repentance. God calls to His children and yearns for their return.

"Return, O backsliding children," says the LORD; "for I am married to you. I will take you, one from a city and two from a family, and I will bring you to Zion. And I will give you shepherds according to My heart, who will feed you with knowledge and understanding. Jeremiah 3:14—15 NKJV

"If you will return, O Israel," says the LORD, "Return to Me; And if you will put away your abominations out of My sight, Then you shall not be moved. Jeremiah 4:1 NKJV

Circumcise yourselves to the LORD, and take away the foreskins of your hearts... Jeremiah 4:4a NKJV

Blow the trumpet in the land; Cry, "Gather together," And say, "Assemble yourselves, And let us go into the fortified cities." Jeremiah 4:5 NKJV

O Jerusalem, wash your heart from wickedness, That you may be saved.

How long shall your evil thoughts lodge within you? Jeremiah 4:14 NKJV

"For My people are foolish, They have not known Me. They are silly children, And they have no understanding. They are wise to do evil, But to do good they have no knowledge." Jeremiah 4:22 NKJV

Go up on her walls and destroy, But do not make a complete end. Take away her branches, For they are not the LORD's.

For the house of Israel and the house of Judah Have dealt very treacherously with Me," says the LORD.

They have lied about the LORD,
And said, "It is not He.

Neither will evil come upon us, Nor
shall we see sword or famine.

And the prophets become wind,
For the word is not in them.

Thus shall it be done to them."

Therefore thus says the LORD God of
hosts: "Because you speak this word,

Behold, I will make My words in your
mouth fire, And this people wood,

And it shall devour them. Jeremiah 5:10–14

Why has this people slidden back, Jerusalem,
in a perpetual backsliding? They hold
fast to deceit, They refuse to return.

I listened and heard, But they do not speak
aright. No man repented of his wickedness,

Saying, 'What have I done?' Everyone
turned to his own course, As the
horse rushes into the battle.

"Even the stork in the heavens Knows her
appointed times; And the turtledove, the
swift, and the swallow Observe the time of
their coming. But My people do not know the
judgment of the LORD. Jeremiah 8:5–7 NKJV

Jeremiah continues with this and we find him mourning for his people — desiring them to repent and return to God. In chapter nine we find the people mourning because of God's judgment against them. This lament continues on and on as God's people break His covenant and stiffen their necks and refuse to return to Him. They even begin to threaten Jeremiah's life — not wanting to hear any more of the Words of God through him as a prophet. The burden on Jeremiah is heavy. He curses that he was ever even born.

But as the book continues, we see that God is moved to restore Israel. Jeremiah prays for healing to come and God promises to restore a remnant. God promises to raise up a Branch of righteousness — a King who will be called, The Lord Our Righteousness.

> *"Woe to the shepherds who destroy and scatter the sheep of My pasture!" says the LORD. Therefore, thus says the LORD God of Israel against the shepherds who feed My people: "You have scattered My flock, driven them away, and not attended to them. Behold, I will attend to you for the evil of your doings," says the LORD. "But I will gather the remnant of My flock out of all countries where I have driven them, and bring them back to their folds; and they shall be fruitful and increase. I will set up shepherds over them who will feed them; and they shall fear no more, nor be dismayed, nor shall they be lacking," says the LORD.*

> *"Behold, the days are coming," says the LORD,*

> *"That I will raise to David a Branch of righteousness;*

> *A King shall reign and prosper,*

> *And execute judgment and righteousness in the earth.*

In His days Judah will be saved,

And Israel will dwell safely;

*Now this is His name by which
He will be called: THE LORD OUR
RIGHTEOUSNESS.* *Jeremiah 23:1—6* NKJV

THE NEW BREED

I have heard many times that the Lord wants us to be childlike. That is true in our trust — childlike faith speaks of absolute trust and confidence. But God expects us to have grown up relationships with Him. I was discussing this with a fellow brother, Joff Day, who has written a wonderful book on the heart and its ability to forgive. In this conversation, Joff was explaining to me that the Lord is expecting us to take greater responsibility for our walk with Him. In a way, we will have to cut a new path and discover new areas and deeper depths of Revelation within the Word of God in order to accomplish what the Lord has asked us to do. Joff explained to me that all the victories are won and we are here as Christians to 'mop up'. He went on to explain that this 'mopping up operation' will begin with the church moving from a place of *knowing* to a place of *inquiring* and that this is the law of motion in action.

Repentance must occur. Institutions created by false doctrine and wrong theology must be disassembled. Fresh inspiration and revelation is being asked for and this is how the nations will be reached. When we return to the first commandment we will love GOD with ALL our hearts, souls and minds. When we love GOD with all our hearts, our ministries will not be competing for attention, glory or merchandising "rights" to the message. He will be glorified and men will cease to feed men, scattering the sheep from the Lord's pasture.

I have not yet witnessed one who has gotten it right. I am not saying that I know the answers or that I have it right either. I do believe that unless we go back and repent for our forefather's mistakes, for our mistakes, and for the mistakes of the church and go to the Lord and ask him to show us the right way, nothing will change. The souls of men are at stake. The Great Commission is at risk. Division and pride keep the body from her true calling.

Division and pride keep the body from her true calling

SETTING GOD'S HOUSE IN ORDER

Before the Lord will judge the earth, He will judge His own house and put it in order. He will rise up a new breed of believer who will not be satisfied with the teachings from memory, built on past doctrines rather than on the Word of God. This new breed of believer will want to know the future of the Kingdom of God on earth, not merely the history of what has happened in churches for the last 2,000 years. Even in the early church, in Ephesus and Corinth there was backsliding, idolatry and immorality.

Yet, even in those days, the finest musicians were gathered to sing and play for the Lord. Praising the Lord was done with excellence — offering God their very best. Why then, when we see excellence and skill in other music today, do we tolerate the bad and amateur in the house of God? We see how the Holy Spirit led composers like Bach, Handel and many others to create masterpieces by His hand. When we look at the mindset of today, we see a Greek philosophy where everything on earth is unholy and what is in heaven is something we need to aspire to. Christian music vs. secular music. This is a double mindset — sacred vs. secular. The Hebrews believed that EVERYTHING was from the Lord. All things were created by God and for God, so there was no category of "sacred" and "secular." Things that are "secular" are merely perversions or misappropriations of God's original intent.

We are not supposed to be of the world — we are IN it, but not OF it. When we are one with God, we have the same authority Jesus did and are able to do the will of the Father. With this purpose and in this authority, we are to take back the world and to redeem it, to take dominion and set it into right order and right standing with God. When we receive the Holy Spirit, we are the risen Christ. We are to be just as Jesus is (and was) on earth. When His bride is fully formed, He will come Himself.

We need to stop for a moment and fully honour the first commandment which says, "I will love the Lord my God with all my heart and all my soul and all my spirit and all my life." Only from there can we proceed as Jesus was, totally dependent on the Holy Spirit all the time. This was His place of fullness and power. That should be our place of fullness and power too. Then the Body of Christ can experience a reformation, doing the works the Father shows.

Jesus only did the works of His Father. He said, "I can of mine own self do nothing: as I hear, I judge: and my judgment is just; because I seek not mine own will, but the will of the Father which hath sent me" John 5:30 KJV. Jesus only did that which God showed Him. We need to be in a place of constant prayer in our hearts, just like Jesus was, and get the Father's attention that He might show us what to do.

Chapter 9

Psalm 23

Nelson says that, "The book of Psalms in the largest and perhaps most widely used book in the Bible. It explores the FULL RANGE OF HUMAN EXPERIENCE."

The Psalms are a collection of 150 songs. These were set to music and played with the accompaniment of stringed instruments. They served as the temple hymnbook and as a devotional guide to the Jewish people.

I particularly want to draw your attention to Psalms 23, a Psalm of David. This was given to David by the Holy Spirit. As the Lord may permit me, I would like to share with you the message that was revealed to me in Psalms 23. To begin, I ask you to read the Psalm in its entirety and then we will divide it into two parts.

The LORD is my shepherd;

I shall not want.

He makes me to lie down in green pastures;

He leads me beside the still waters.

He restores my soul;

He leads me in the paths of righteousness

For His name's sake.

*Yea, though I walk through the valley
of the shadow of death,*

I will fear no evil;

For You are with me;

Your rod and Your staff, they comfort me.

*You prepare a table before me in
the presence of my enemies;*

You anoint my head with oil;

My cup runs over.

Surely goodness and mercy shall follow me

All the days of my life;

And I will dwell in the house of the LORD

Forever.

Psalm 23 NKJV

~~~~~~~~~~~

The LORD is my Shepherd. The word Shepherd, in Boyd's dictionary, is defined as a herder of sheep. In Bible culture, the office of sheep master or chief shepherd was one of great trust as well as honour. He led the flock to pasture in the morning, tended them by day and saw them safely back to the fold where he watched over them at night.

In the New Testament, all references containing the word shepherd refer to Jesus. It is the Lord Jesus who is the Good Shepherd. Jesus cares for us — leads us to

the place where we can be fed (good pasture), tends
to all our needs and leaves us wanting for nothing.

> *He leads me beside still waters. He*
> *restores my soul. He leads me in the paths*
> *of righteousness for His name's sake.*

How does He do this? How does He cause us to
lie down by still waters in a place of refreshment
and peace? How does He restore our soul?

In John 14, Jesus promised to send us a helper, the
Holy Spirit.   He promised that this helper would abide
with us forever and that this Spirit would dwell IN us.

In the Gospels we read that Jesus breathed on
the Apostles and said, "Receive the Holy Spirit." In
the second chapter of Acts, on the day of Pentecost,
we read that they were all together in one room,
waiting for the promise of the Lord. We read that
Holy Spirit fell on them and filled them. The Baptism
of the Holy Spirit is available to every believer and
has been available to us on the earth — having the
capacity to live in us, since just after Jesus died
on the cross and left the Comforter with us.

The Holy Spirit is the Comforter. He is part of the
Trinity and has a divine personality. He is the bringer
of gifts and the worker of miracles that point to Jesus
— Holy Spirit always points to Jesus — the Shepherd.

Jesus is the Shepherd. He dwells in us (with the
Father and the Holy Spirit). With His heart, He will
make sure that we do not lack anything. He will make
us lie down in green pastures and rest and He will
lead us to the still waters of refreshment and peace.

The still waters by which he leads them yield
them, not only a pleasant prospect, but many a

cooling draught, many a reviving cordial, when they are thirsty and weary. God provides for his people not only food and rest, but refreshment also and pleasure. The consolations of God, the joys of the Holy Ghost, are these still waters, by which the saints are led, streams which flow from the fountain of living waters and make glad the city of our God. God leads his people, not to the standing waters which corrupt and gather filth, not to the troubled sea, nor to the rapid rolling floods, but to the silent purling waters; for the still but running waters agree best with those spirits that flow out towards God and yet do it silently.[1]

He restores our soul with His presence and His Word He leads us in the paths of righteousness for His Name's sake.

In verse four, David talks about the walk through the valley of the shadow of death. Most people are familiar with this valley. It is dark and the way is unsure and too often we are filled with fear. Here, David tells us that even though we WILL walk through this valley — we need not fear evil. We have His rod and His staff to comfort us.

How does this bring comfort? Many times in life we are tested and not just by people and events, but sometimes the test is from the enemy — taunting us and trying to deceive us. Tests by people challenge us to walk in forgiveness, and challenge us to put "love they neighbour as thyself" into practice. (Which, according to Scripture, is equal to the first commandment.) Tests by circumstances or events challenge our faith and make us ask "why me?" Tests by the enemy

---

[1] Taken from Matthew Henry's Commentary on the Whole Bible: New Modern Edition, Electronic Database. Copyright © 1991 by Hendrickson Publishers, Inc.

challenge our faith and cause us to doubt in the power or protection of God. The Shepherd's rod (or staff) was used to direct the sheep — keeping them from wandering away from safe paths, and also to protect them from enemies — wielding blows to predators.

You prepare a table before me
in the presence of mine enemies.

Many times, I have seen the enemy march against the man of God — often by attacking members of his own family. These enemies accuse and torment, they stir up strife and bring questions against their credibility. Sometimes one who was once close to them will even turn against them, saying things like, "Oh, you will never do that," or, "He will never stop smoking and drinking." They may attack with lies like, "He will never amount to anything. He will never have a penny. He is a failure."

But God says that He prepares a table for us right in the midst of these enemies. The table is a place of provision and blessing. It is a place of God's favour and abundance. So, when your enemies rise up against you like a flood, God will come in. He will prepare His table of blessing and provision and invite YOU to come and dine!

He anoints my head with oil; my cup runneth over.

The word Christ means "Anointed One," and He that anoints you. He baptizes you with His spirit and with fire and anoints your head with oil. An anointing is a "smearing." When a King was anointed, the oil marked him as the one set apart. When God anoints you — you are marked as one set apart unto Himself. Even the enemy recognizes this mark and understands the authority placed on you by the One making the mark! Now — your cup runs over with God's power. Philip Byler, an apostle and friend, teaches that the anointing gives you permission to handle the glory of God, with the confidence to trust His grace. The anointing of God is powerful.

Surely goodness and mercy shall follow me All the days of my life.

In the Sermon on the Mount (Matthew 5:8), Jesus says, "Blessed are the merciful for they shall obtain mercy." Here, David tells us that we will have that mercy all the days of our life. What a glorious promise! The Psalm concludes with, "And I will dwell in the house of the Lord forever."

This Psalm is God's heart toward us. When we receive His heart and walk with Him, with our hearts quickened to His and living in prayer, this is exactly what He will give us. Jesus said, "Pray constantly, that you shall not fall into temptation" Mark 14:38 NKJV. We must have a prayerful heart which is constantly glorifying, worshipping and thanking God. He is pleased when we worship Him in secret — in the private place of our closet when no one can see us and say how "spiritual" we are. Being in constant prayer doesn't mean that we whisper prayers all day long — it means that even when we don't speak words of prayer out loud, God will know it when our hearts are turned toward Him and He will answer us.

Chapter 10

*"Prayer is as natural an expression of
faith as breathing is of life."*

Jonathan Edwards

*"Nothing penetrates the human heart as does a
personal, fervent prayer and its heaven—sent response."*

Thomas S. Monson

I cannot tell you how to pray. In fact, I do not
want to tell you how to pray, for if you try to pray by
a set of rules or by a formula, you will miss the beauty
of discovering how to express yourself to God. What
I want to do, is to encourage you and tell you that
you can walk and live a life which is closer to God.

Most of what has been taught on Jesus today has
centred on His ministry before the cross. Most people
get to the cross and just stay there. We need to look
at the ministry of Jesus on earth today, after the cross.

When we believe and know that Jesus died for us on the cross, we aren't supposed to acknowledge it for today and forget about it by tomorrow. How many of us would behave differently if it was our son or our father or someone with whom we were in deep relationship with hanging on that cross? Yet, Jesus died for us. Our relationship with Him should be our most valued possession. His sacrifice for us should move us deeply.

I tell you now, most of us are guilty of coming to the Lord in the most casual way. We walk into our houses and the Lord has been there, but we just put on the television and turn our backs on Him — day after day after day. With our faith drifting into oblivion, we find ourselves in need, and instead of going to God, we run to another man and ask him to pray for us. "Oh, Pastor so and so, I did this, I lost my temper, I lied to this person, I don't pray any more, I've no money to pay my bills, etc." Sound familiar?

Wherever you are, this is the moment to get down on your knees in front of God and say;

> *"Father, I repent. I am so sorry. I want to start a new life with You. I want to walk with you every day. I am sorry that I have allowed myself to trust and rely on other people to feed me and pray for me, when You have been there all along waiting to reveal to me Your heart and give it to me, each day. From the moment I wake up until the moment I go to sleep, teach me to walk in Your ways, with Your wisdom and Your understanding. I forgive all those who have harmed me, and I ask You to forgive me for everything I have ever done. Jesus, I am sorry for ignoring you, and your Holy Spirit, please forgive me. I want to return*

to the moment when you saved me and start
again from there in a new relationship with
You. I want to have You as the head. Amen."

FORGIVE QUICKLY

I want to offer you this — forgive quickly. Forgive all those who have hurt you. Be unyielding with your forgiveness. Be tough on your own flesh, even as Jesus was. The quicker you forgive, the less chance you will give Satan to have place in you.

When we love God and forgive those who have hurt us, we are in a place of perfection, in His eyes. Jesus said, "Be perfect, therefore, as your heavenly Father is perfect" Matthew 5:48 NIV.

Be imitators of God, therefore, as dearly
loved children and live a life of love,
just as Christ loved us and gave himself
up for us as a fragrant offering and
sacrifice to God. Ephesians 5:1–2 NIV

In Ephesians, we read the writings of the Apostle Paul. As you come to chapter three of the Book of Ephesians, I want you to personalize the following passage and make it your own.

Beginning with "*...how that by revelation He made known to me* **(put your name here)** *the mystery ...by which, when you* **(put your name here)** *read, you* **(put your name here)** *may understand my knowledge in the mystery of Christ, which in other ages was not made known to the sons of men, as it has now been revealed by the Spirit to His holy apostles and prophets:" Ephesians 3:3–5 NKJV*

I pray that you will stand on the prayer Jesus prayed for all of us (and the apostles). That He will come to dwell in your hearts and that you (your flesh) would decrease as He increases in you. Allow His word to gather substance in you so that what is built in you is built by God as you follow in obedience. There are various levels of understanding the scripture. And there are various levels to experiencing the depths, the breadths, and the heights we can know if we allow God to dwell within us. The levels are opened up for us according to how deeply we give life to His word.

Therefore, I believe that there are various levels of power and also various levels of authority attached to those levels of power. These levels of power and authority are attributed according to the size and presence of spiritual wisdom and understanding attributed to each facet of each level. This is demonstrated in the amount of fruit that we bear in the Spirit.

I pray that your eyes and ears may be opened and the wisdom of God may fill your heart. I leave you in the presence of the Lord.

Chapter 11

Gateway to the Promised Land

The word authority means that we have been given the right to exercise power. Authority is associated with power, ability and influence. When one has authority — they have license, they have been sanctioned to do a particular thing or they have been given a mandate, permission or authorization.

Authority deals with government and the power of rule. Those who are subject to authority must obey the will and commands of those who are IN authority — exercising their power.

The word power means strength, force, or ability. God's strength is manifested in His right hand — the hand of power, the place where Jesus is seated. Paul speaks of this in Ephesians, Chapter One:

"...that the God of our Lord Jesus Christ, the Father of glory, may give to you the spirit of wisdom and revelation in the knowledge of Him, the eyes of your understanding being enlightened; that you may know what is the hope of His calling, what are the riches of the glory of His inheritance in the saints, and what is the exceeding greatness of His power toward us who believe, according to the working of His mighty power which He worked in Christ when He raised Him from the dead and seated Him at His right hand in the heavenly places, far above all principality and power and might and dominion, and every name that is named, not only in this age but also in that which is to come.

And He put all things under His feet, and gave Him to be head over all things to the church, which is His body, the fullness of Him who fills all in all. Ephesians 1:17—23 NKJV

Christ is seated at the right hand of the Father. This is a place that is above all principality and power, above all might and dominion, a place that is above every other name. A place where ALL things have been put under His feet. The amazing thing about this is that WE are supposed to be seated WITH Him in this place!

But God is so rich in mercy, and He loved us so very much, that even while we were dead because of our sins, He gave us life when He raised Christ from the dead. (It is only by God's special favor that you have been saved!) For He raised us from the dead along with Christ, and we are seated with Him in the heavenly realms — all because we are one with Christ Jesus. And so God can always point to us

as examples of the incredible wealth of His
favor and kindness toward us, as shown in all
He has done for us through Christ Jesus.

Ephesians 2:4—7NLT

When we receive Christ we are born again. And
then we are, "buried with Him in baptism, in
which you also were raised with Him through
faith in the working of God, who raised Him
from the dead" Colossians 2:12 NKJV.

We need to ask God to create the inner man in us from the heart of Jesus outwards. We also need to ask Him to give us His eyes, His ears and His mouth. We need to ask Him to dress us in His amour and give us His understanding of the Word so that we CAN BE SEATED AT GOD'S RIGHT HAND and realize that authority and power every moment of every day of our lives.

We must ask Him to greatly multiply the fruit of the Spirit which can be found in Galatians 5:22. These are the keys that unlock the Gateway to the Promised Land. You will find them listed below:

Love
(as Christ has also has loved us)

Joy

Peace

Long—suffering

Kindness

Goodness

Faithfulness

Gentleness

Self—control

When these keys are formed, and as the fruit matures, we will have grown up relationships with God. We will be entrusted with more than we have ever seen before in our walk with God. Our prayer lives should be focused on the development of our relationship with God.   We must be concerned with the construction of the inner man, and receiving the heart of God, Jesus' heart. But we must also be concerned with receiving these keys and allowing this spiritual fruit to develop and mature. We must pursue the unlocking of wisdom and understanding in the Kingdom of Heaven as when Jesus died for us and the Gateway to the Promised Land was thrown open.

Chapter 12

~~~~~~~~~~

The Kingdom of Heaven

The word heaven is used commonly and casually in our vocabulary. People use the word "heaven" to describe any *place* or *state* that is pleasurable or filled with good fortune. Someone takes a mouthful of delectable chocolate cake and says, "I'm in heaven!" Another looks at a pretty girl and says, "I must be in heaven!" But heaven is much more than a mental image or state of physical pleasure — heaven is a very real place. Heaven is more real than this earth. Everything on this earth will pass away and turn to dust, but heaven is eternal. We have seen sparks of it descend on this earth when we look at Jesus, who came from heaven, and consider that what He left behind is still alive and functioning to this day. What He left behind is the Holy Spirit and the miracles that continue to manifest as a result of His promise and power.

We have seen men and women, sick or deformed, touched by heaven and miraculously healed. We have even seen some who have died and, after being touched by heaven, have been able to rise and walk — alive once more. And these miracles are only a glimpse into the very beginning of this place called heaven. It is the place where we will live forever, as Jesus said, "But whosoever drinketh of the water that I shall give him shall never thirst; but the water that I shall give him shall be in him a well of water springing up into everlasting life" John 4:14 KJV.

When the Holy Spirit is active in us and we have been graced with an anointing, we see the Lord looking at us and we know in that moment that we have been given authority in a certain point in time to accomplish a certain thing God shows us and wants us to do or obey. The angels are looking at us and are waiting for their commands and in that moment we actually feel heaven all around us and over us.

HEAVEN

The word heaven comes from the Hebrew word, *shamayim*. I want to look at this in more detail. I want to share some of the descriptions of heaven and the levels (or layers) of heaven (or the heavenlies) that are spoken of in God's Word. I also want to acknowledge that I gleaned most of this information from studying heaven using Strong's Concordance.

Layer One

"...and let birds fly over the earth in the open expanse of the heavens. Genesis 1:20b AMP

This is a description of the first layer of the heavenlies. It is the realm of the sky, where birds fly. It is the place that is just above the surface of the earth.

Layer Two

The LORD will send rain at the proper time from his rich treasury in the heavens to bless all the work you do. Deuteronomy 28:12 NLT

The second level of the heavenlies represents an area farther removed from the earth's surface. It is the place of the windows of heaven from which precipitation comes.

Layer Three

And when you look up into the sky and see the sun, moon, and stars — all the forces of heaven — don't be seduced by them and worship them. The LORD your God designated these heavenly bodies for all the peoples of the earth. Deuteronomy 4:17 NLT

Shamayim also represent the realm in which the sun, the moon and the stars are located. This would be beyond earth's atmosphere — it would be considered the firmament. *(See also Genesis 1:14, Psalm 104:2, Isaiah 34:4).*

Layer Four

*In the beginning God created the heavens
and the earth. Genesis 1:1 NLT*

The phrase "heaven and earth" is thought to
denote the entire creation — the totality of the
whole. This would represent both the known and the
unknown universe in its totality. The verse below
represents an example of this "unknown" universe.

*David looked up and saw the angel of
the LORD standing between heaven and
earth with his sword drawn, stretched out
over Jerusalem. 1 Chronicles 21:16 NLT*

Layer Five

This fifth level is the dwelling place of God

*He who sits in the heavens shall
laugh... Psalm 2:4 NKJV*

*Therefore know this day, and consider it in
your heart, that the LORD Himself is God
in heaven above and on the earth beneath;
there is no other. Deuteronomy 4:39 NKJV*

*Indeed heaven and the highest heavens belong
to the LORD your God, also the earth with all
that is in it. Deuteronomy 10:14–15 NKJV*

The Kingdom of Heaven

In the last chapter, I described the keys that unlock the Gateway to the Promised Land — the Kingdom of Heaven. And now that you have the keys, you must find the actual locks for unlocking. The secrets to this place can found in the Sermon on the Mount in Matthew 5.

It begins with "Blessed are the poor in spirit for theirs is the Kingdom of Heaven." As we ask the Lord for more of his Spirit, the Holy Spirit and His presence, the heavens are opened from that moment forward. The blessings that proceed are all visited upon us from heaven.

The sermon continues;

"Blessed are those who mourn, for they shall be comforted."

"Blessed are the meek, for they shall inherit the earth."

"Blessed are they who hunger and thirst for righteousness for they shall be filled."

"Blessed are the merciful for they shall obtain mercy."

"Blessed are the pure in heart for they shall see God."

"Blessed are the peacemakers for they shall be called sons of God."

"Blessed are those who are persecuted for righteousness sake, for theirs is the Kingdom of Heaven."

"Blessed are you when they revile and persecute

*you and say all kinds of evil against you falsely
for my sake. Rejoice and be exceedingly glad,
for great is your reward in heaven, for so they
persecuted the prophets who were before you."*

The Kingdom of Heaven is the place of blessing. It
isn't a place filled with material wealth — cars or money
like we know. Those things are here on earth. But before
I discuss what we will find in heaven, I want to emphasize
that the kingdom of heaven is the place of blessing.

When a man is healed, he has been touched by
heaven. When a man receives the supernatural gift
of wisdom and knowledge, he has been touched by
heaven. When someone is born again, he has been
touched by heaven. When a man receives the Holy
Spirit, he has been touched by heaven. All blessings
come from the One in which all good thoughts
originate from His will. His dominion is heaven
and He is Father, God. He desires to bless. He
desires to give. He desires us to live in the Kingdom
of Heaven. Jesus said that unless a man be born
again he shall not see the Kingdom of Heaven.

So in the sermon, every time Jesus says the
word "blessed," the blessing is from the kingdom
of heaven and it begins with the man knowing that
he is poor in spirit, ready to receive from God.

There is much to study regarding the heavens
and the Kingdom of Heaven. I do not want to
overwhelm you with words and definitions. Rather,
I desire that your heart will be pricked and that you
will be compelled to discover the joys of heaven on
your own. Pray that the eyes of your understanding
will be open and boldly ask God to reveal Himself

to you. He will do it! He will speak to your heart and unwrap His mysteries when you desire Him.

Below is a scripture that I have prayed for years. I would personalize it, putting my name in place of Peter's. I have taken it from the Amplified Version of the Bible and I want you to try it. Pray this scripture. Put your name in the scripture and make it personal between you and God.

2 Peter 1:1—8 AMP

SIMON PETER **(your name)**, *a servant and apostle (special messenger) of Jesus Christ, to those who have received (obtained an equal privilege of) like precious faith with ourselves in and through the righteousness of our God and Savior Jesus Christ:*

May grace (God's favor) and peace (which is perfect well—being, all necessary good, all spiritual prosperity, and freedom from fears and agitating passions and moral conflicts) be multiplied to you in [the full, personal, precise, and correct] knowledge of God and of Jesus our Lord.

For His divine power has bestowed upon us **(me)** *all things that [are requisite and suited] to life and godliness, through the [full, personal] knowledge of Him Who called us* **(me)** *by and to His own glory and excellence (virtue).*

By means of these He has bestowed on us **(me)** *His precious and exceedingly great promises, so that through them you* **(I)** *may escape [by flight] from the moral decay (rottenness and corruption) that is in the world because of* *covetousness (lust and greed), and become sharers (partakers) of the divine nature.*

For this very reason, adding your diligence [to the divine promises], employ every effort in exercising your faith to develop virtue (excellence, resolution, Christian energy), and in [exercising] virtue [develop] knowledge (intelligence),

And in [exercising] knowledge [develop] self–control, and in [exercising] self–control [develop] steadfastness (patience, endurance), and in [exercising] steadfastness [develop] godliness (piety),

And in [exercising] godliness [develop] brotherly affection, and in [exercising] brotherly affection [develop] Christian love.

For as these qualities are yours and increasingly abound in you, they will keep [you] from being idle or unfruitful unto the [full personal] knowledge of our Lord Jesus Christ (the Messiah, the Anointed one).

Like Peter, when my heart was right, God has bestowed upon me all things that are requisite and suited to life and godliness, through the FULL, PERSONAL KNOWLEDGE OF HIM — Who called me by and to His own glory and excellence. It is possible for you to experience this same divine power from God. Position yourself to receive from God. Posture yourself to be transformed by His spirit. Allow Him to replace your old heart with His and your spiritual eyes will be opened.

Finding the Kingdom of Heaven

Nicodemus, a respected ruler of the Jews, came to Jesus one night asking Him about the signs and wonders He performed. Jesus answered him that a person had to be born again from above if he were to experience (and be acquainted with) the Kingdom of God (Kingdom of Heaven).

Now, Nicodemus had no knowledge of salvation and being born again (literally) seemed impossible. He asked Jesus how could a man be born again once he was already old? Jesus replied with solemn assurance that unless a man is born of water and the spirit he cannot ever enter the Kingdom of God. What is born of the flesh is flesh, and what is born of the Spirit is Spirit. This truth remains for us today.

When we receive Jesus in our hearts and ask Him to fill us with the Holy Spirit, we receive the Kingdom of God — the Kingdom of Heaven, and it comes and lives in us. Wow! From this Kingdom (where God the Father, the Son and the Holy Spirit live), are all things given to us. This place is linked by a thread which is the actual dwelling place of God. Our heart is the only place where man can move between these two worlds and this is because of the Holy Spirit.

When we ask for the Lord's heart to be placed within us, our heart will always be one with Him. When Jesus came to bring Heaven on earth, His heart was always one with the Father. When we have His heart in us, it means that we will also always be one with Him and the Father together with the Holy Spirit.

Distractions

Many of us wake up in the morning and what do we do? We feed our flesh to stop our tummies from rumbling. We sit down and a magazine catches our eye. Before we know it, the television is on and we are hearing about things we should buy — things to make us look better, smell better and feel better. We watch news that is filled with disaster and crime and unrest. In fact, when was the last time you watched the news and heard only good things? Have you ever turned on the news channel and heard a reporter saying, "Mr. So and So was healed of this... This amazing woman is doing good works here... Many people were reported to have received blessings and gifts from this place....?"

No, all we hear about are disasters, economic stress and political corruption. When we become bored of it all or are tired of the strain, what do we do? We pull out a DVD or go out to the movies. Just the pressures and responsibilities of every day life can even be a strain. We check the mail only to find bills and we wonder how we will pay them. We get tired and are filled with stress and anxiety. Sometimes, we even get angry.

So where is God? We have squeezed His presence so far away that we can't even find Him anymore. If we want to live a victorious life filled with purpose and joy, we have to give

If we want to live a victorious life filled with purpose and joy, we have to give God our whole hearts

God our whole hearts. From the moment we wake up until the time we go to bed, we must ask for the heart of Jesus to be put in us and to grow. Only then will we know the fullness of God. Only then will we experience His promises and live in His blessing. Only then will we walk with purpose and fulfil our destiny.

WHERE IS YOUR TREASURE

The Lord has shown me that He only allows us to walk and exercise power and authority in the areas which we have been given permission to operate. This is extended or granted to us by the measure of our wisdom — as God sees it. This can also be granted according to the fullness of our walk, even if our understanding is somewhat lacking but our heart is pure and open to the Holy Spirit's leading.

For where you treasure is there will your heart be also. Matthew 6:21 KJV

THE FINAL VISION

As I close this final chapter of the book, I want to share with you what the Lord showed me as he appeared to me in a vision. The date was 19 August 2005, and the vision was given at 11:00 AM. He told me to write it down and that when I did, this particular message on the heart would be complete.

I was taken up to Heaven in a moment!

I was sitting on the ground under a tree with my back to a wall. Passing from the left to the right was a path (in what appeared to be grass) which was cut short and well tended. On one side of the path, about 5 meters away, was a hedge made up of trees running parallel to the path.   To my right was what I can only describe as a fortress — about a 1,000 meters away. The sun was shining on me and as I looked up from where I was sitting, the Lord was standing in front of me. He was dressed in white. The sun shone through His hair and He shone in the light.

His voice was comforting but firm. "Are you ready to listen to Me always?"

I stared at Him. His voice went into me and found its place to hold me. I looked down and the place was my heart.

Are you ready to listen to Me always?

Again He asked me, "Are you ready to listen to Me always?"

He was smiling, and the words went into me like a sword. I looked up at him and I said, "Yes!" And tears swelled in my eyes.

He said, "Look down, here. These stones you have walked on, making up this path, have become your life. They are your promise to Me — to walk them, and in walking them, they are My promise to you."

It was hard to take my eyes off the Lord. (I had first seen the Lord in a vision that occurred nearly seven years before, but I had not seen all of Him.) This time I could see His face, His skin, His eyes...everything. I looked at the stones that

He was pointing to. They were like stone tablets.
They were very old. "Older than the earth," He
said to me. The Lord was answering my thoughts!

As I looked at these stones I could see that they
had names on them and the names were of the
Apostles who wrote the Gospels. I couldn't make out
everything, as my eyes were constantly drawn back to
the Lord and then again to the stones. I looked more
closely. The stones were alive. They were revealing
scripture, which was alive. The stone had a column
or margin in which names were being scrolled from
top to bottom in what seemed like an endless list.

I was sitting on the floor under this tree and the
Lord then said to me, "Now look to your right under the
tree."

I stared down at the base of the tree and saw
all these hats scattered there. They were like
baseball caps. The Lord spoke, "Many have fashioned
weapons to fight for me on earth, but have put on
one of these caps. The enemy persuades them
to put them on when they are not attentive."

I looked at one of these hats closely and
saw that they all had the same name written
on them, the name said – *Distraction*.

The Lord spoke again, "Are you ready to listen to me
always?"

I said, "Yes, my Lord."

The Lord said, "Then what shall you do from
here?" as he pointed to the entire place in the
vision. He moved his right hand from left to right.

I said, "I am waiting."

He said, "And why are you waiting?"

I answered, "I am waiting to be shown what I must do now. For I am here only for you, Lord."

"Then I will show you something," said the Lord.

Here we started to fade, and I saw different places in the earth — I saw cities. I saw people who had written daily diaries and though I wasn't sure who had written the pages, I now know that it was the enemy. These people were naked, and as I looked closely at them, I saw that their flesh was rotting. Their eyes were sown shut. Their ears were sown shut. Their mouth were sown shut and on their backs was a sign that read, *"No Inner Man."*

The Lord then took me for a walk down a street. We stopped outside the front of a church and went in. Nobody saw me and nobody even noticed the Lord. The Lord was standing next to me and pointed up at the roof. There was no roof. Instead, there was an angry sky and a tornado going down to hell in the centre of the building. The Lord's hair was blowing in the wind and He said in a raised voice next to my ear, "The enemy lives here now. All those who come in here are lost."

I saw the same deaf and blind people walking past us. I stared as they walked straight past the Lord. Next to each one of them, there were creatures like dark shadows, reading their diaries to them and writing on papers which were all being sent down to hell in the tornado. The pages of the diaries were filled with events and sins from within these people's souls. Even the confessions they had made which were heard by priests and ministers were there — condemning them.

The Lord said to me, "Let us leave this place." And I

couldn't wait to go.

We walked out of the door and came to place where there was a big range of mountains. I saw a big stage that was hundreds of meters wide and there were more of these rotting corpses — deaf, blind and dumb, walking about. There were grotesque looking women wearing only jewels and stones, their flesh rotting away. Lights were turned on them, and they were mumbling through closed lips and were being filmed.

The cameraman and directors were also rotting and were deaf, dumb and blind. These sad cameramen were being manipulated — like marionettes, by a big, dark creature that I could not see. They were all smiling at one another and mumbling through closed lips an undecipherable, meaningless, speech.

The Lord pointed up to the top of the mountains above this vast stage. I saw that there were some letters there, each one about ten meters high. Some had fallen and some had nearly dissolved. I looked hard and then I could make out at the end of the large word, an "O" and then another "O" and part of a "D." You could just make out the beginning of the supports for the letter "H" that made up the word "HOLLYWOOD."

We left that place and now the Lord was standing with me above the clouds. We looked down and zoomed in to a gathering where there were thousands of people. The Lord said, "I like him. Watch this."

I saw a man on earth that I recognized — I mean I know his name, he was an evangelist. Behind him were two massive angels. They were the biggest angels I have ever seen, (I believe them to be Throne Angels). They were over four or five meters tall, and were standing behind the man. They had their arms folded in front of them and were waiting. The evangelist was standing and talking to the people. When the angels both touched him (one on each shoulder) laying their hands on him, their wings opened out and started to move. It was then I saw the ball of light beginning. It began in the place where the man's heart is and it became bigger and brighter until his whole body was made of light. Then the Lord said, "Now, watch this!"

The two angels turned round and looked at the Lord. They saw me standing next to him. Jesus then lifted His hand and put it down to His side. The light shone out from the man — the evangelist. It shone first from his heart and then from his eyes, his mouth and ears and finally the whole body became a jet of light and shot out like lightening. It went through everyone there, thousands of them — right through the place where their heart is. They all now had opened ears, opened mouths and opened eyes and were glowing from the inside and balls of light were now in the centre of their chests. At that moment, thousands of bat—like creatures flew out of the crowd into the sky forming a dark cloud, which lifted and moved away.

The Lord looked at me and smiled. He was standing to my left, and as I turned to face Him, He put His right hand on my left shoulder. I put my right hand on His left hand. His hand felt warm — soft but full of energy. The third finger of my right hand was touching an impression below the centre of the forearm just under the wrist bone. It was then I saw the hole in his hand under the wrist, the Lord looked straight into my eyes and at that point my heart started to see the place where my salvation was won. The tears came flooding from my eyes and as I looked down, they fell and they stopped in midair.

Without transition, we were suddenly in a room of *gold*. In this room there were many chests of golden, steel—like material. The room was revolving around us, but my tears were suspended in time, they still had not reached the floor. There were so many chests that I could not count them. The Lord looked into my eyes and said, "This is the Room of Treasure in Heaven. Where your heart is, there your treasure shall be also."

Each chest had a different name written on the lock. The Lord opened one which said JOY, and so much joy went into me I could not contain it. The same thing also happened when He opened the chest marked LOVE. When He opened this one, I was in a state of euphoria and could not contain or even describe the feelings I experienced. There simply are no words in existence on earth.

The room, the walls, the paths, and each stone in the floor all had scripture written on them and were alive. Even the Lord's voice was constantly speaking in scripture to me, it was as if the Word of God was flowing out of my own heart from within and He was answering my thoughts — all while having a normal conversation with me.

I did not want to leave Him. He turned around and started to walk out of the room and down a corridor. I ran after Him. He turned back to look at me over His shoulder and I cried, "I don't want to leave here. I want to be with you always!"

I don't want to leave here — I want to be with You always!

He answered and said to me again, "Are you ready to listen to me always?"

I shouted, "Yes, Lord!"

Then I was back in my home, sitting down in my bedroom and the same tears that were falling from my eyes hit the floor. The Lord's voice came to me and said, "You have got your piece of heaven, keep it in your heart — the heart I gave you. It will be the heart that will touch the lost because it is full of Me and My word. It is the heart that has some of Me in it, and carries some of this place inside. This heart is all that can reach some of these people — before you can ever even give them My Word. Some of them are so controlled by the darkness that they run away when they hear the Word. The Kingdom of Heaven is within you, use it! I came to bring it on earth. Use what you have been given. I will be watching. Are you ready to listen to me always?"

It was then that I remembered that the Word of God is sharper then any two edged sword. The moment I spoke that out in my spirit, I saw a two edged sword, and then two men in front of me. In one man's hand was a sword, so sharp it was like a scalpel and it shone in the light. In the centre of his chest I saw in the place where his heart was, melted gold and fire.

In the other man's hand (who stood next to him and was half in darkness) was a sword that was rusty and bent and decaying. His heart was darkened and I could detect no life in it. I turned to my left and saw an angel standing next to me — he was shining. He was about three meters tall and had eyes all around his head. He also had a face with two eyes and looked at me. I said to him, "What use is a sword like that?" (I meant the rusted one and somehow, I was not afraid.)

All of a sudden the man started waving the sword and it broke in half. His words were jumbled up scripture.

I said to the Angel, "False teaching, was it?"

The Angel said, "The Word is not in his heart, but don't tell him that. His pride will put what's left of that sword at you and hit you with it. So many are doing that these days. Foolish men are even trying to point this feeble "weapon" at the Lord to get what they want down here, you know?"

"How can this change?" I said.

"Well, you change it. That's why you are here," said the Angel, "Isn't that why you have been shown the truth?"

The Lord was next to me again. He looked into my eyes and said, "Move with My times and seasons. Rest when I rest you, drink when I give you drink, eat when I feed you, and speak when I open your mouth. The Spirit will show you and give you the words you are to say. Do not fear. Do not be troubled, for I am with you always, even unto the end of the age."

AN INVITATION

Finally, To anyone who is reading this book, I want to say that there is a reason you are reading this. If you are not saved — you have never been born again, then now is the time! You must be born again and receive the Holy Spirit. It will cost you nothing. Its free and it is God's greatest gift. It will be the most wonderful and exciting thing that you could ever do. It will be the beginning of a great adventure. Cleave to the cross of Jesus and then ask for His heart to be given to you. Within His heart is the Kingdom of Heaven, His presence and a wonderful walk with Him. He is waiting for you. Pray this prayer and scripture below.

Ezekiel 36: 25 - 30

25) "Then I will sprinkle clean water upon you and you shall be clean from all your uncleanness and from all idols (the self and its vain imaginations we are to cast down, the created image and other gods) will I cleanse you.

God, I acknowledge You as Creator. I believe you sent Your Son to die for my sins. Cleanse me from my sin — I receive this cleansing.

26) "A NEW HEART WILL I GIVE YOU AND A NEW SPIRIT, (a new quest and divine personality) WILL I PUT WITHIN YOU AND I WILL PUT AWAY, THE STONY HEART OUT OF YOUR FLESH AND GIVE YOU A HEART OF FLESH.

God, give me this new heart and new spirit. Give me a heart of flesh for my heart of stone.

27) "And I will put My spirit within you and cause you to walk in My statues and you shall heed My ordinances, (creations) and do them.

God, I receive Your spirit. I desire to walk in your statutes and fulfill my purpose.

28) "And you shall dwell in the land that I gave to your fathers and you shall be My people and I will be your God.

God, I desire to dwell in the land and be yours.

29 "I WILL SAVE YOU, from all your uncleanness AND I WILL CALL FORTH THE GRAIN (provision) and make it abundant and lay no famine on you.

God, thank you for saving me from unrighteousness. I embrace your abundant provision and rejoice in your protection.

30) "And I will multiply the fruit of the tree and the increase of the field that you may no more suffer the reproach and disgrace of famine among the Nations."

God, thank you for harvest and increase. Thank you for lifting me above reproach and disgrace and blessing me among the Nations.

A MESSAGE TO BELIEVERS

I want to encourage you to take a season of time where you focus on talking TO the Lord Jesus instead of talking ABOUT Him (or about doctrine or theology). When you have a relationship WITH someone you don't spend all your time talking ABOUT them — you talk TO them. Spend more time with Him. Love Him with all your heart. Yes, there is a price to pay for deep communion with God. You will have to invite Him in with your whole heart and mean it. You will have limit distraction and idle pursuits and be willing to spend time alone with Him. But — the price is worth the reward. The reward is unity with God. Unity with God will give you the ability to walk in the same authority Jesus had and do even greater works than He did.

Matthew 7:21–23 warns about "empty" Christians who will profess that they have known Him, but have never truly walked with Him. Do not be among these who know everything about the church and about programs and doctrines but have never tasted true communion with Christ. Know God.

> *"Most assuredly, I say to you, he who believes in Me, the works that I do he will do also; and greater works than these he will do, because I go to My Father. And whatever you ask in My name, that I will do, that the Father may be glorified in the Son. If you ask anything in My name, I will do it. John 14:12–14* NKJV

ACKNOWLEDGEMENTS

I would first like to thank, the LORD JESUS
for saving me and giving me His heart.

I give thanks to my beloved wife, ERIKA, for her
patience and understanding as I was creating this work.

I acknowledge the following people for
their contribution to my understanding,
in their encouragment to me for the
completion of this manuscript and for their
dedication to God and His Gospel.

Apostle John Kelly

Joff Day and Victor Lorenzo
Vision of the Future

Debbie Holmes

Stephen Bennet

Kenneth Hagin Ministries

Wendy Walters

BIBLIOGRAPHY

I acknowledge the use of the following
publications and eagerly recommend them to you.

Forgive and Release
by Joff Day: Sovereign World Publishing

The New Strong's Exhaustive Concordance of the Bible
by James Strong: Nelson Reference & Electronic Publishing

Vine's Concise Dictionary of the Bible
by W.E. Vine: Nelson Reference &
Electronic Publishing

Boyd's Bible Dictionary
by James P. Boyd: B&H Publishing Group

The City of God
by Saint Augustine of Hippo: Random House Publishing

The Dead Sea Scrolls
by Michael Wise, Edward Cook & Martin Abegg:
HarperCollins Publishers

The Gracious God — Gratia in Augustine and the 12th Century
by Aage Rydstrom-Poulsen: Akademsisk Forlag, Publisher

Matthew Henry's Commentary
by Matthew Henry: Hendrickson Publishers, Inc.

Unless otherwise noted, all Scripture
references are taken from:
New King James Version of the Bible
Thomas Nelson Publishers

BIOGRAPHY

Esteban Antonio

Quoted as one of the greatest guitarists of our century, Esteban Antonia began to study both Flamenco and Classical styles of the guitar at three years of age.

At the age of nine, he was the youngest guitarist to get into the Royal College of music in Kensington London. He was the youngest guitarist in the world ever to perform the Concerto Aranuez by J. Rodrego. He did this at only eleven years of age and performed it again in Oxford with the County Youth Chamber Orchestra in 1977.

At age 18, he toured Japan, performing in 40 concerts throughout the nation. When he was 20, he began touring Europe and played in France, Germany, Italy, Holland, Finland and Denmark. Then at 30 years of age, he began touring America and Canada, including Quebec and Montreal.

Esteban has worked with Juan Paredes and Jose Ortega, Cristina of Hoyos Company, George Michael, Johnny Depp and many others. He has worked with Sony Records, EMI, Miramax Films, among others.

Esteban has done extensive recording, including four film soundtracks. One of them received the award for best music for short film at the Cannes Film Festival. He has recorded and composed 80 different album projects, and is also a composer and producer. In addition, he is an accomplished acoustic as well as electric guitarist and plays all styles of guitar.

In 1997, he had a traumatic accident in which he irreparably damaged his spine at the s1, s2, and s3 vertebrae. This caused the loss of feeling in his legs and then partial immobility with limited movement was made possible by huge doses of drugs. It was impossible to fix by any conventional means. His continued use of painkillers began to destroy his internal organs until the Lord Jesus Christ showed up in London, Victoria. God supernaturally straightened Esteban's spine — growing two centimeters of bone in just seconds! Many were present to witness this event. At that moment, Esteban gave the Lord Jesus his life. He was born again and filled with the Holy Spirit.

This book, From Heart to Heaven. has been written to bless you. It is born from the fires of adversity that have created a passion for the Lord in Estaban. His desire is that God would transform your life like He did his life in 1988.

"I gave away everything I had to follow the Lord. I have had my battles and my ups and downs, but the Lord has always brought me through. He's blessed us with new music, a life changing ministry, finances, power and the greatest gift, to serve Him and bring light to the nation of Spain."

Esteban travels extensively, but resides in Spain with his beloved wife, Erika and their child. To learn more about Esteban and Erika's vision and passion to reach people with the transforming power of God's love, visit www.savespain.org or www.whitehorseministry.org.